the sacred art of
BOWING

the sacred art of
BOWING

preparing
to practice

Andi Young

Walking Together, Finding the Way
SKYLIGHT PATHS Publishing
Woodstock, Vermont

The Sacred Art of Bowing:
Preparing to Practice

First Printing 2003
© 2003 by Andi Young

For information regarding permission to reprint material from this book, please mail or fax your request in writing to SkyLight Paths Publishing, Permissions Department, at the address / fax number listed below, or e-mail your request to permissions@skylightpaths.com.

SkyLight Paths would like to thank Jennifer J. Wilson for her assistance with this book.

Library of Congress Cataloging-in-Publication Data
Young, Andi, 1980–
The sacred art of bowing : preparing to practice / Andi Young.
p. cm. — (Preparing to practice)
ISBN 1-893361-82-9
1. Posture in worship. I. Title. II. Series.
BL619.P67 Y68 2003
204'.46—dc22
2003014938

10 9 8 7 6 5 4 3 2 1
Manufactured in the United States of America

SkyLight Paths Publishing is creating a place where people of different spiritual traditions come together for challenge and inspiration, a place where we can help each other understand the mystery that lies at the heart of our existence.

SkyLight Paths sees both believers and seekers as a community that increas-ingly transcends traditional boundaries of religion and denomination—people wanting to learn from each other, *walking together, finding the way.*

SkyLight Paths, "Walking Together, Finding the Way" and colophon are trademarks of LongHill Partners, Inc., registered in the U.S. Patent and Trademark Office.

Walking Together, Finding the Way
Published by SkyLight Paths Publishing
A Division of LongHill Partners, Inc.
Sunset Farm Offices, Route 4, P.O. Box 237
Woodstock, VT 05091
Tel: (802) 457-4000   Fax: (802) 457-4004
www.skylightpaths.com

To all my teachers, thank you.

CONTENTS

INTRODUCTION
WAKE UP!

Bowing (also called kneeling, prostrating, or genuflecting) was not always an important part of my spiritual life. In the relaxed Lutheran household in which I grew up, we rarely prayed, and at church I just knelt when the pastor said to kneel. I didn't have a strong connection to the Lutheran Church or to Christianity in general. I also didn't know at the time that other Lutherans and Christians were engaged in interfaith dialogue and were opening to other traditions to explore their own faith. My parents allowed me the freedom to explore other religious and spiritual traditions, and so even though I went through First Communion and Confirmation in the Lutheran tradition, I was always looking to other traditions to help me understand myself and my world. When I was thirteen, I read *The Miracle of Mindfulness* by Thich Nhat Hanh, a Vietnamese Zen Buddhist monk. Wow, I thought—meditation! This was something new to me, and helpful. I would wait until my parents went to sleep and the house was quiet, and then I would bunch a pillow under me and sit cross-legged, just like Thich Nhat Hanh said to do in his book. Just by sitting still, my mind felt more still. Not entirely still, but definitely less crazy than usual.

I meditated on and off throughout high school and read a little about Buddhism. But I had never met a living teacher, gone to a Buddhist temple, or meditated with other people. Consequently, I thought that Buddhism was *only* meditation, just sitting cross-legged on a pillow and counting my breaths. When I got to college, however, I found other people who studied and practiced Buddhism, and I learned more about Buddhist philosophy and gained practical experience meditating. For my first two-and-a-half years at Yale, I would go to the Zen Center in New Haven from time to time, maybe once a semester. I also sat occasionally with the Buddhist Society on campus. At both the Zen Center and the Society, meditation practice always began with a bow. I chalked this up to something cultural, inherited from the various Asian cultures in which Buddhism first took root. Even though I bowed, I did it sort of mindlessly, not really attaching any significance or larger purpose to the action.

When I was a junior in college, I took a semester off from school and traveled to Nepal. The four months I spent in Nepal were exhilarating and terrifying months. I found myself in an unknown country and culture, surrounded by the dust and color of Katmandu, its grinding poverty and hospitable people, Hindu temples, and Buddhist stupas (reliquaries) everywhere I looked.

While in Nepal, I began to seriously study Buddhism. Then, as I started attending teachings, going to temples, and spending time at meditation centers, I began to understand that meditation was an important, but not the only, part of Buddhist practice. At the recommendation of my teachers, I started chanting and bowing in addition to sitting meditation.

I found that each aspect of practice—sitting, chanting, and bowing—was another tool to help me calm and focus my mind. My mind needs so much help! Sometimes sitting felt like turning up the volume on all the voices in my head, worrying about this or that and chasing after thoughts, creating elaborate fantasies and scenarios, rather than focusing my mind and calming my thoughts. I needed a tool to help me work with my busy mind. A teacher of mine said that if you have a mind that won't sit still with your body, try doing extra bows.

So I began to bow. I felt somehow *right* when I bowed. The three bows when I entered a temple or left a temple, the bows before the teacher and the altar, and then the series of bows I did on my own, in sets of one hundred and eight, all felt right. My mind was no less chaotic when I bowed than when I sat, but *doing* something was like finding a big hand-hold on a rock wall where before I had only found small finger-holds. I found I was able to let go of my chaotic thoughts a little more easily when I was bowing. Now, even when I sat, instead of turning up my mind's volume, I could turn it down. Bowing requires as much concentration as sitting meditation does. The physical motion, however, gives the mind something on which to focus. After bowing, I felt a little calmer, a little less scattered, more focused. Of course, I often rapidly lost that focus after bowing practice, but the best part of practice is that you can always come back to it.

When I first moved into the New Haven Zen Center, I was in my last semester of college. I had some late nights, a lot of deadlines, a job, and now a full practice schedule at the Zen Center. I managed to get up most mornings, though not all, for practice at 5:00 A.M. The morning always began with one hundred and eight bows. Even when I couldn't stay awake through the morning meditation (sometimes I just went back to bed—what use was I falling asleep on the meditation cushion?), I tried to get up for bows.

In the midst of my busy student life, I found that bowing not only helped me focus my mind, but also helped me stabilize and ground myself each day. The physicality of the practice, the motion and the rhythm of bowing, helped me wake up when I might have otherwise fallen asleep, both physically and mentally. "Enlightenment" is only one way to describe what the

Buddha attained after his night spent under the bodhi tree in India 2,500 years ago. He also "woke up," and that is what *Buddha* means, "the awakened one." What the Buddha awoke to was the nature of reality, and to his own innate wisdom and compassion. So bowing has been and remains for me a way to wake up each day, to connect with my *own* Buddha-nature, my wisdom and compassion.

In my talks with other people about their bowing practices, I've found that bowing is how many people "wake up" in their spiritual life. Bowing is a spiritual practice that uses the body to awaken the mind and spirit, across traditions and forms. Each day, Christians, Muslims, Jews, Hindus, and many other people from different spiritual backgrounds bow as part of their spiritual practice. They may begin their day by bowing, or they may bow at specific times and places. This book explores the many forms and traditions of bowing. I hope that in reading this book, you will find ways either to deepen or to begin your own bowing practice and can "wake up" to your own spiritual potential. Whether you are calling on divine aid, reflecting on the human spirit, or attaining enlightenment, bowing can help you.

So wake up!

CHAPTER ONE

BOWING AS
A SPIRITUAL PRACTICE

The floor is cold under my bare feet as I stand, palms pressed together and centered at my heart. Incense drifts in faint wisps across the dharma room, and I can smell its sandalwood and juniper smoke. Outside, the half-light of predawn gives the rows of cushions blue shadows. It is 5:00 A.M., and the residents of the New Haven Zen Center—myself included—are up for morning practice.

We begin with the Four Great Vows:

Sentient beings are numberless; we vow to save them all.
Delusions are endless; we vow to cut through them all.
The teachings are infinite; we vow to learn them all.
The Buddha Way is inconceivable; we vow to attain it.

After the recitation, we do a half-bow from the waist. Then we begin our daily practice of one hundred and eight bows. We begin standing, our hands pressed together in a prayer position called *hapchang* in Korean. Then, keeping synchronized with the head dharma teacher, I bend my knees until I am kneeling on my meditation mat. I bring my hands down to the front of the mat so that I am kneeling on all fours. Tucking my right foot under my left, I bring my forehead to the mat between my hands, and I turn my palms upward. All of us pause here for a moment, then rise up onto our hands and knees again, then rock back onto our heels, place our hands in *hapchang*, and stand. We do this together, in silence and synchronicity, one hundred and eight times in the chill blue light.

Daily, across America and across the world, people begin their day by bowing. Christians kneel for morning prayers, Muslims turn east to Mecca for the first *salat* (prayer) of the day, Jews *daven* (pray), and Buddhists prostrate themselves. Over the course of the day, many more people will find time to pause and, bending their body toward the earth, bow as part of their spiritual practice. Each spiritual tradition has its own way to bow, yet despite the seeming difference between Catholic genuflection and Buddhist prostration, traditions share the common need to express their aspirations, ideals, and faith in the physical act of bowing.

But what *is* bowing? A great diversity of forms and names exist for so simple an idea—that of a physical posture people use in their spiritual practices. In western Christianity, bowing differs greatly between Roman Catholics and Protestants, even to the degree that many Protestants might not recognize some of their physical actions during services and prayer to be akin to the acts of bowing, genuflection, and prostration used in the Catholic Church. While a greater similarity exists in forms used in the Eastern Orthodox Church and the Roman Catholic Church, both churches maintain distinctions between their respective forms. When we begin to examine the prayer postures of Jews and Muslims, even greater differences arise in the way bowing is performed and named according to different traditions. And when we expand our view even further and look at Buddhism, from South Asia to the Far Eastern countries of Korea and Japan, the idea of bowing as a unified practice among traditions begins to dissolve with the sheer diversity of forms, names, and purposes within each spiritual practice.

Yet the fact that such a great diversity and multitude of traditions have given a place to and maintained the practice of bowing—however named or performed—only brings home the necessity of studying and understanding bowing, in all its variety. Bowing, in its simplest terms, is a change in physical attitude, usually meant to indicate humility and respect. All religions specify moments during formal worship and ritual when we should punctuate our inner state with physical action. Bowing is intimately connected with the ways in which we cultivate our faith and our hearts, because bowing is never meant as an empty gesture, to be done without awareness or intent. Instead, bowing is meant to call us to greater awareness of our thoughts, emotions, and intentions.

Because tradition, although important and central to the continuation of religion and spirituality, can also inspire dogmatism and closed-mindedness, it is important to remain as open to other traditions' theologies and philosophies as it is to be open to other forms of bowing outside of our own experience. And because bowing looks different from tradition to tradition, how we define bowing must remain somewhat fluid and able to adapt to the intention we perceive and experience behind actions, either our own or others'. In this spirit, we can consider even a simple lowering of the head, when done with great awareness, humility, and intention, to be bowing.

Often, bowing is integrated with formal prayer. Muslims pray five times daily, and the spoken words and the bowing of the body are considered one practice, that of *salat*. In Judaism, at specific passages in the daily prayers, those praying bend their knees and lean forward in *davening*. When I was a child and attending my parents' Lutheran Church, we kneeled at certain parts during the service or bowed our heads with the rest of the congregation to pray. Prayer and bowing seem to fit naturally together. Our feelings of humility, repentance, submission, and gratitude find their best expression in more than words.

We may also bow suddenly, in the haste of immediate need or inspiration, without forethought or ritual. Physical movement, from the full-length prostration of a Tibetan Buddhist who places his or her entire body on the ground to a simple lowering of the head, calls our attention to our actions and our intentions. As we change our posture, we become more mindful of our emotions. Why are we bowing? Are we angry or sad? Joyful, thankful, or awed? The moment that we take to shift our bodies is also a moment to shift our perspective away from the mundane and toward the divine or exemplary. As we begin to bow or pray, our awareness and focus gives us the opportunity to open our hearts, to the Divine or to ourselves, and clarify our intentions. Do we wish to express humility? Are we thankful, and seeking to express that thanks? Are we asking for aid, to overcome inner or outer obstacles in our lives?

Bowing is more than a connection between our inner state and our outer posture, however. Because bowing is physical, it is *beyond* words and thoughts. Often, when we are unable to articulate our feelings, we turn to movement to express ourselves. The words for our feelings—joy, despair, gratitude, or sorrow— are only words. How we express these emotions is the great question of ritual and worship. Bowing is one answer to the question of how we can express our spiritual aspirations; yet, even among spiritual practices, bowing stands alone in its sheer physical nature. Our movement becomes its own purpose, and, at times, our need to articulate drops away and we can make our bow itself a prayer and an aspiration.

Different spiritual and religious traditions share common ground in the general purpose and use of bowing in rituals and personal practice. Each tradition, however, also has a unique bowing form, a specific relationship between how and why we bow, and a philosophy and theology of that tradition. In exploring bowing in different traditions, we also have to explore a little of each tradition's history and thought. The way in which each tradition relates the individual to the Divine, and its study of that relationship, has great impact on the purpose that forms the way in which people practice.

There are many more traditions in the world than can fit in one book about bowing, so I have chosen to explore the major world religions and the main divisions—if any—within each religion, rather than attempting to include every religion, tradition, and sect that exists. Often, despite differences in doctrine within a given tradition, the purpose of bowing remains constant, and world religions have more in common than in difference when it comes to practicing faith. With the goal of looking closely at bowing in several traditions, I have chosen to explore bowing in Buddhism (and Zen in particular), Judaism, the Christian traditions of the Roman Catholic and Eastern Orthodox Churches, Islam, and Hinduism.

These religions have often persecuted one another, either through violent physical punishment and exile or through the more damaging insistence that there is one and only one "truth"—and this community or that faith has it and others do not. Still, in studying religion, spirituality, human suffering, and human faith in our better selves, I found it hard to hold onto my belief that my own tradition and practice was "it," the only truth out there. Rather, as I began to understand the common ground all traditions share, I began to see that I could learn from those whose faith and tradition were different from mine. My own practice as a Buddhist has deepened as I have talked and shared with Jews, Christians, and Muslims. I met a nun in a local Catholic parish who had lived in Japan for ten years, working with the Catholic community there. While in Japan, she studied Zen and still carries her experience of bowing in the Zen tradition with her into her Catholic faith, and she feels a stronger relationship with God because of her Zen bowing practice many years ago. I spoke with a rabbi who explained to me that, according to Judaism, humanity is still able to take part in God's creative process because humankind was made in God's image and likeness. While humanity often acts in violent and terrifying ways and is capable of the most horrendous actions, each person also carries within himself or herself the capability for great compassion and healing. When we get too heady with our importance, our bowing before God reminds us that we are not to act for ourselves alone, but for the whole world. Such humility and generosity of spirit—with or without belief in God—is something toward which each of us can aspire.

At the heart of bowing is *practice:* consistent effort over time. In order for bowing to benefit us and our spiritual practice, we must be disciplined and consistent in our efforts. My personal practice is centered on Buddhist meditation and philosophy. I have the unique advantage of living in a Zen center, which is extremely beneficial for me, because discipline is not one of my strong points! For me, living in a Zen center motivates me to make time for practice every day, and living and practicing in a community setting helps me find support and inspiration in my fellow practitioners. Practicing with a community also gives me access to resources for my questions and struggles.

Finding or strengthening your own connection with a community can be a vital part of your own spiritual practice. For some, such a connection is more necessary than it is for others. I know many Zen masters, Christian monks, and students from all religious sects who don't ever need to step into a temple, church, or holy place to find their inspiration and strength. But if you, like me, need a little help, finding a community can motivate you to develop a practice. Having regular times for practice, access to someone who can answer your questions, and the support of others can provide stability for your personal practice at home.

Bowing as a practice, rather than as part of a practice, is a unique and challenging aspect of any spiritual path. Buddhism is unlike other major world religions (with the exception of Hinduism) in that bowing is a practice unto itself, not just part of a ritual or performed at specified times. Buddhist history is full of stories of practitioners, both laypeople and monastics, for whom bowing *was* their practice. One

Chinese monk, Empty Cloud Zen Master, bowed three thousand miles across China. Tibetan Buddhists aspire to make the pilgrimage to sacred Mount Kailash in Tibet and perform the thirty-two-mile-long *kora,* or circumambulation, which is done by prostrating around—and often on the way to—Mount Kailash. Two American monks from the Chinese tradition completed a "three steps, one bow" journey of one thousand miles along the California coast in 1973 and 1974.

Examples and stories abound in contemporary Buddhism, and in contemporary spirituality. I hope that bringing you some of these stories, and the stories of others outside the Buddhist tradition who have found inspiration and guidance for their own spiritual practice in the Buddhist model, will help you either begin or deepen your own bowing practice.

FROM KATMANDU TO CONNECTICUT

I first encountered bowing as a spiritual practice when I began studying Buddhism in Nepal. Initially I studied Tibetan Buddhism, but when I returned to the United States, I began going to the New Haven Zen Center in Connecticut, near where I lived. In practicing at the Center, I found Zen helped me focus my mind.

The New Haven Zen Center is part of the Kwan Um School of Zen Buddhism, which came from Korea with our founding teacher, Zen Master Seung Sahn, a Korean monk. Zen Master Seung Sahn (also called Dae Soen Sa Nim, or "great honored Zen teacher") brought Korean Zen to America in the 1970s. With him he brought Korean forms and customs that he and his first students adapted to the West and Western customs.

Dae Soen Sa Nim didn't change bowing, however. Bowing is central to a balanced Zen practice, along with chanting and sitting meditation. As in other traditions, we bow at specific times during the daily liturgy, and we also bow when entering or leaving the meditation hall. Because the meditation hall is a space specially set aside to help people attain enlightenment, bowing when we enter and leave shows respect for our own and other people's efforts to attain enlightenment. We also bow to the Buddha on the altar, not because he is superior to us, but because we, like the Buddha, have Buddha-nature, or the potential to "wake up" and attain enlightenment.

Bowing is also a formal and concentrated practice. In Zen temples across the world, the day begins with one hundred and eight bows. We bow in repentance for our bad actions, things we have done that were selfish, hurt other people, and hurt ourselves. When we bow, we have the opportunity to say, "I'm sorry," but that doesn't mean developing guilt about our bad actions. Repentance does not mean we bow, feel guilty, and then don't change our negative attitudes and actions. In America, we hear a lot about karma, which only means "action" in Sanskrit. When we act, we also produce a result. Good actions, such as helping others, produce good results in our lives. Negative actions produce negative results. Although karma means "action," the idea behind the word is the interplay of these good and bad actions and their results. We can change our karma by changing our mental and physical actions.

Often, we act out of habit. Sometimes the habits have good intentions, sometimes negative. We often get stuck in a selfish habit, where we consider our own needs first and as being more important than the needs of others. We create negative karma this way, by consistently acting out of selfishness. We hurt other people when we act without care for them, and then we get in the habit of thinking and acting for our benefit alone. Breaking mind habits is hard. They're like addictions. We're used to our mental habits, and they feed our ideas of ourselves. We constantly think, "*I* want, *I* need, *I* deserve." When we think like this, our sense of "I" gets strong, and it's hard to think about the needs of others. Our minds become rigid and stiff, always thinking "I, I, I." This kind of thinking both is and creates our karma. We developed the "I" habit in the past, and by thinking, "I want this, I don't want that," we set the ground for the habit to continue in the future. We also set the ground for suffering in our own lives, because when we are selfish and unhelpful to those around us, they mistrust and dislike us.

I've heard many American students of Buddhism say that bowing was one of the hardest practices for them to do. In America, Buddhist-style bowing—knees, hands, and head on the floor—is unusual, so for Americans bowing is a particularly difficult practice. We may think, "*I* don't bow like that; I don't want to put my head on the floor for anyone or anything." This is our mental habit of "I" coming up, which is why Dae Soen Sa Nim always reminds his students that we are not bowing for ourselves, but for others.

When we bow for others, we acknowledge that we have created negative karma because of our selfish mental habits. This is the repentance part of bowing, when we say, "I'm sorry." By acknowledging our negative actions, we begin to bend the stiff attitude of "I, I, I" and make it more pliant. As our minds become more flexible, we loosen our attachment to ourselves and to our needs. If we can say, "I'm sorry," then we can also begin to think not just "What can I do for myself?" but "What can I do for you?" Our small minds, the minds that think only about themselves, get bigger, more open, more aware and compassionate. Then our bowing practice creates momentum to act in our everyday lives.

As I said earlier, bowing in Zen is not about beating yourself up. As you bow, you don't think, "Oh, I'm such a terrible person! I'm selfish and bad. I must bow because I'm such a bad person." This is still attaching to the "I." Guilt is self-indulgent. Repentance means saying "I'm sorry" not just to the people you have hurt, but also to yourself, for trapping yourself in a cycle where your negative actions create hurt and mistrust all around you. When you're motivated by selfishness, you make yourself suffer by creating a bad situation.

Zen is about understanding our minds and waking up. So when we do our one hundred and eight bows, we have an intention: to let go of our small minds so we can help others. The immediate meaning of bowing is repentance, but the deeper understanding underlying bowing is the two aspects of enlightenment, *prajna* (wisdom) and *karuna* (compassion). Wisdom is letting go of our small mind (or "small I," as Dae Soen Sa Nim calls it), which is limited and attached, and attaining our "big I," which correctly perceives its true nature. Compassion is asking, "How can I help you?" Wisdom and compassion work together. When we understand that our selfishness and attachments hurt other people, we feel compassion for their suffering. And our compassion turns into action, every day asking, "How can I help you?" and *meaning* it, so that if helping is getting a sick person a glass of water, standing up to a bullying coworker or friend, or letting go of our anger toward someone so that neither we nor the other person is hurt by that anger, we just do it.

But we shouldn't think too much about bowing. All the symbolism and meaning involved in bowing is just explanation; bowing, really, is *just bowing,* putting our hands together and bending our knees. Bowing with one hundred percent awareness is waking up to bowing in that moment. When we wake up one hundred percent, then compassion and wisdom are already present.

Bowing in Zen is physical. I often break a sweat trying to keep up with Zen masters during morning bows. I also lose track of how many bows I've done, because I'm so easily distracted— which is why I keep showing up, morning after morning! Bowing is a *practice,* something we do to train our minds and open our hearts. We all start somewhere, and I started with a chaotic and confused mind. But I find it harder to get distracted by my thoughts when I'm trying to concentrate on my bows. I also find it harder to feel arrogant or angry when my forehead is on the floor and my hands are palm up to the ceiling or sky. I once asked one of my teachers, Zen Master Barbara (Bobby) Rhodes, why we bow. She asked me in return, "What do you feel when you bow?" I replied, "I feel humble." She told me that we place our hands palm up, in a gesture of surrender and receiving, so that we can receive the teachings of the whole world. These teachings are that our original mind is wise and compassionate and that we can wake up for the benefit of all sentient beings.

Zen does not tell us to believe in something or someone outside of ourselves to help us wake up. Zen asks that we believe in our own potential to be wise and compassionate. When we bow at other times in the meditation hall, such as when entering or leaving, and when we bow to the Buddha statue and to our teachers, we are bowing to the ability of all beings to wake up. We show respect to those who have experienced insight into their own minds and who have taught us, because in respecting their experience we also respect our own experience. The Buddha was the first teacher, and he gave us the mind-to-mind transmission of his "waking up" in an unbroken lineage clear to the present day. Ultimately, bowing in Buddhism and in Zen is a physical manifestation of our aspiration to practice compassion and attain enlightenment.

My bowing practice began on the other side of the world, in Katmandu, Nepal. When I was a junior in college, and feeling restless with the intellectually exciting but viscerally dull world of academia, I decided to take a semester off and travel. But where? I decided not to go on any "study abroad" programs, because formal studying was the last thing I had in mind. I had always wanted to go to Asia, however. And I was a little curious about Buddhism. A few times each semester, I would attend either a small student-led sitting meditation group or go to the Zen Center in New Haven. But I didn't really absorb much information about Buddhism there. I mostly got sore knees from not being used to sitting on a meditation cushion, and a vague sense that I wanted to learn more. But I never had the time to learn more. I had other books to read, papers to write, and tests to study for. My curiosity, however, got stronger the more I thought about traveling to someplace where there were lots of Buddhists. I wanted adventure, too, and an exotic location to which many people hadn't been.

I chose Nepal. Lumbini, the birthplace of the Buddha, lies just inside the Nepali border with India, and I thought the country holding the birthplace of the Buddha was as good a destination as any. The closer I got to leaving, the more I forgot my interest in Buddhism and the more I felt the excitement of going somewhere new and strange. I was also eager to leave behind a disastrous semester at school. I hadn't performed too badly grade-wise, but I was leaving behind a bad relationship and some big mistakes. I wanted to run away from everything, and Nepal was about as far as I could geographically get without leaving the earth.

Immediately upon arriving in Katmandu, I realized I was unprepared for the shock of another country. Katmandu was sprawling and dirty, the Himalayas obscured by the thick pre-monsoon dust that hangs in the air above the Katmandu valley. At the airport, a business contact of a family friend met me to take me to a hotel. I was thankful; without Gombu, I would have been completely lost, as well as probably fleeced by a taxicab driver while trying to get to Thamil, the tourist district where all the hotels were.

When Gombu, who was holding a sign with my name on it, saw me coming toward him, he pressed his hands together at his heart and bowed slightly toward me. "*Namaste,* welcome!" he said. This was my first lesson in bowing. In Nepal, and in India as well, *namaste* is a word used for both greeting and parting, and it is always accompanied by a small bow with the hands held in *anjali* ("prayer position," in which the hands are held, palms together, at the heart). A flowery translation of *namaste* is "I salute the Divine in you." While I'm not sure everyone, including myself, holds this meaning in their hearts every time they shout *"Namaste!"* to neighbors across the street or friends in a market-place, I do know that as I became used to greeting both strangers and friends in this manner, I felt friendlier toward others.

Americans don't bow in social situations; we reserve bowing for religious situations, usually, and occasionally proposals of mar-riage (at least in the fairy-tale scene with which many of us grew up). But bowing, all the time and to anyone who even happened to catch my eye, was a powerful shift in the way I saw my rela-tionship to everyone around me. Men I didn't even know would call out, "Hey, *didi, namaste!*" They were saying, "Sister, hello!" And I would answer back, *"Namaste, daiju!"*—"Hello, elder brother!" The forms of address and greeting in Nepal were all familial, and at least in theory, if not always in practice, showed deep respect. For a strange *injee* (white) woman in Katmandu, I was always aware of the language I was using and the actions I was performing, because they weren't a habit to me yet.

Then I started going to visit temples. I was so shy. I didn't want to offend anyone. I would creep into the courtyard, and often creep back out without having even gone into the *gompa,* or meditation hall and main altar space. I would usually go to the Boudhanath Stupa, a reliquary, outside of the Katmandu city center. I watched and watched everyone around me. Every morning and evening, the whole community—many of whom were Sherpas, Tamangs, Gurungs, and other ethnic groups from the Himalayas, and some of whom were Tibetan refugees—would come out and circumambulate the stupa, turning the prayer wheels, chanting mantras, or even catching up on gossip with their friends. The stupa had several tiers. The outer circum-ambulation path had a high wall with prayer wheels set into it. The next path, just inside the outer wall, had along it big wooden boards, almost like rectangular tables without legs all facing toward the center of the stupa. When I first saw these, I didn't know what they were.

But as I continued to come to Boudhanath, I saw people using the boards to do Tibetan-style full prostrations. Ah! Now I understood. People came to do prostrations, usually in sets of one hundred and eight. The full and new moon, as well as other auspicious holidays, were the peak times for people to come and do prostrations. Offering prostrations at a stupa or some other holy place was meritorious. Sometimes, if people didn't get there right away in the morning, around 6:30 or 7:00 A.M., a board wouldn't be free to use until nearly noon, when the heat made prostrating difficult.

A full-length prostration is a physical experience. With your hands in *anjali,* you touch them to your forehead, lips, and throat, then come down to your knees and hands. From there, you slide your hands up and stretch out your body until you're completely on the ground. Usually, although not strictly, you then put your hands in *anjali* again above your head before sliding back on your palms to kneeling, and then up to standing. To see a hundred people all prostrating at once made me realize what kind of commitment many Buddhists had to their practice.

I also watched people go to the *gompas.* They would enter and do three half-prostrations, which begin the same as a full prostration, but instead of stretching out, they just press their foreheads to the floor while kneeling, then stand up. As I became less shy and met a few people who spoke English and could tell me it was okay to go into the *gompas,* I crept all the way up to the doors. I wasn't sure how I would feel about prostrating once I went in, but I also believed that "when in Rome, do as the Romans do," so I was unwilling not to show the necessary respect by prostrating. I stayed in the doorway of the temples, and I watched the people go in and out.

All this time, I had been reading about Buddhism, going to teachings, and talking about Buddhism with different people, including my friend Gombu. He is from a small village in the

Solu-Khumbu region of Nepal, famous because Mount Everest lies within its borders. Gombu is a funny and articulate man. He's been to the United States many times and had gone to church with his American friends on numerous occasions. He takes a broad view when it comes to religion—whatever helps an individual be a better person, find peace, and help others is the best path for him or her. So I could talk a little with him about Buddhism, because he understood my own background to a sufficient degree that he could draw parallels to my religious experience in Christianity.

I also met American students studying in Nepal, some of whom were "dharma brats," or the children of the first American students of Buddhism. They had grown up around monks and temples, meditation and bowing. They also understood, even better than Gombu, the questions I had about Buddhism and American culture.

I gradually grew less awestruck by the strangeness of the *gompas* and the prostrations, and more inspired by the idea of enlightenment. I finally got around the doorframe of the temples, and I would make a few hasty prostrations and then scoot over to the side to watch the monks and the laypeople that came to make offerings. My favorite *gompa* in Boudhanath was right off the main circumambulation path. It was small, in terms of floor space, and dim like most of the *gompas,* because it didn't have any windows. But it did have a huge, three-story-high gold statue of the future Buddha Maitreya. Every time I saw it, I was struck with the urge to prostrate. Faith, and gut-level action without thinking, was still beyond me, however. I was caught up in my mind, asking, "What does it mean if I do this, why would I do that, what is this Buddhism? I don't like feeling like I'm venerating a statue. Meditation is hard; it's boring. I like the idea of it, but really . . . it's too much work."

Meanwhile, everything I had been running from back home caught up with me, mostly in my heart. All my mistakes, and all the people I had hurt, hit me hard. I suddenly understood that I had been acting selfishly, so selfishly, without concern for anyone around me. I had even acted without concern for myself, doing things that I really didn't want to do but had done because I felt as if I needed to prove I was a certain kind of person: edgy, daring, and revolutionary.

One evening, I went into the *gompa* to listen to the evening prayers. The monks were filing in and out, sitting down and getting ready. I was exhausted from carrying around my guilt and sorrow. My heart hurt, in a literal way. In my chest, I had an aching and suffering place that I couldn't get rid of, because it was a place that felt—even as I was still struggling with understanding—my own selfishness and my own accumulated actions. I couldn't get rid of it because every action we do stays with us in some way. This is karma, and I couldn't just wish my karma away. I made three prostrations right when I got in the door, then I walked up to the statue of Maitreya.

The Buddha Maitreya is not a savior figure like Jesus is. Buddhism sees time as endless and believes this world will be destroyed at some point and another world system will arise. The Buddha of this age, the historical Buddha Sakyamuni, is the seventh in a line of Buddhas belonging to a long age called a *kalpa*. Time is beginningless, composed of *kalpa* after *kalpa,* and endless. The next Buddha who will come is Maitreya. Currently, Maitreya is a Bodhisattva who waits in heaven for his time to manifest in the world of living beings and establish Buddhism for the benefit of all sentient beings. The Buddha Maitreya is usually depicted sitting as if in a chair, with his hands held up in a gesture called the teaching mudra (gesture). He wears a crown, showing that he has not yet achieved full Buddhahood but is on his way.

In the *gompa,* I stopped before the statue of Buddha Maitreya. It is a beautiful statue, inspiring because of the grace and serenity conveyed on Maitreya's face. I had read enough to understand that the Buddha and all the Bodhisattvas were examples every person could follow to attain enlightenment. Each quality of a Buddha or Bodhisattva, be it wisdom, compassion, purity, action, or keeping vows, is a quality each human being already has. I looked up at Maitreya, and I thought, "I've been too selfish to ever be like *that!*" And I burst into tears.

One of the monks, uncertain what to do with a crying *injee,* sort of hovered and then just left me alone. I cried and cried, silently, and then, not really thinking, I made three prostrations. I did them slowly, and with great intention and awareness. They were powerful prostrations for me. They came not from some thinking, analytical part of me that didn't want to put my head on the cold and dusty floor, or venerate a statue, or try and find some other way of repenting, a swap for guilt. The prostrations weren't an exchange. I couldn't trade my guilt for a dusty forehead and call it even. But I could *repent,* which isn't guilt. Prostrating was a letting go, a willingness to say I'd made a mess of things and I couldn't think my way out of it because I was stuck in my same old mind habits. In repenting, I found I could begin to work with my situation in a productive way. I could say, "I made a mistake, now how do I make amends and move forward in a responsible way?"

After that evening in the *gompa,* I felt a close connection to prostrating. I started going to more teachings and listening to the teachers, and when I entered the *gompa* I made my three prostrations with joy. Prostrating became my way to connect with my gut feelings and let go of my thinking mind. Of course, I still had to figure out the mess I had left behind in America, and no amount of prostrating was going to erase the events and people I had left and to whom I would have to return. But prostration became my turning around from a selfish and unaware life toward one with greater awareness and compassion. I'm still trying, and every day I have to turn around. One of my teachers, Acharya Judith Simmer-Brown (a student of the Tibetan teacher

Chögyam Trungpa Rinpoche), talks about life as a constant letting go. It's not that we become detached from life—we're actually always becoming attached. We just learn to let go.

For one of the full moon holidays, I decided to do five hundred prostrations. That was an experience! I found a prostration board early in the morning. I set up my knee and hand pads, and I started. Because the ground was muddy, I had left my flip-flops on so that I wouldn't have to stand in the mud at the end of my board. The woman next to me noticed this, and she stopped me. "No shoes," she said, and she handed me a scrap of cardboard, so that I could place it under my feet instead of wearing shoes. She was very nice and helpful, and just wanted me to do the prostrations right.

After I did about two hundred, my arms were tired, I was sweating in the humid air, and I was out of breath. I noticed that some older women were walking around the prostrating people and handing out flat little cakes and paper cups full of sweetened milk tea. I could hear them discussing me as they came closer to my board. I caught the word *injee* several times, and being the only white person at the stupa, I understood quickly that they were debating whether or not to offer me the bread and tea. I didn't know enough Nepali to understand the specifics of the conversation, but when they got to my board they graciously offered me bread and tea with warm smiles, and I was thankful for the food!

As the sun rose and the crowd around and on the stupa grew, I felt a little conspicuous. People gathered on the tier above the people performing prostrations. I felt as if they were all watching the strange white woman, although that probably wasn't the case. I was worried I wasn't doing my prostrations properly. After all, I had left my shoes on for about fifty prostrations; who knew what else I wasn't doing right? I tried to concentrate on the mantra I was reciting, *Om Mani Padme Hum.*

I can't remember if I actually completed five hundred prostrations. Around 11:00 A.M., the sun was high and hot and people were packing up and leaving for home or for the teashops that ringed the stupa. I packed up as well. I was exhausted. But I left feeling looser and more open. Most of us carry around a tightness in our minds and hearts. We don't think much about it because it's always with us, and very little can touch this tightness in a way that reveals it to us. I wasn't used to moving my spine that much, either. While standing, walking, and sitting, I'd always kept my back straight, which is good for posture but not for flexibility. All that bending and bowing loosened up my spine, and with my body my heart and mind loosened, too.

I came back to America after four months in Nepal. I worked over the summer and got ready to go back to school in the fall. Before I left Nepal I spent about two weeks at Kopan Monastery outside of Boudhanath, going to teachings and meditating. Kopan Monastery is the home of Lama Zopa Rinpoche, who was traveling and not at the monastery when I was there. I wanted to continue to study with his community when I returned to the States—but the closest center in his school was all the way up in Boston. I sat with some friends, and it was relaxed and informal. But I wanted something formal. I was hungry for hard practice and guidance. Now that I had studied a little, experienced sitting and prostrations and chanting a little, I wanted more.

Getting up to Boston on a regular basis when I had a lot to do and didn't have a car was difficult. So when the school year started and the group I had been sitting with over the summer dissolved, I started going to the New Haven Zen Center. It wasn't Tibetan Buddhism, but it was formal practice and a nice temple and residence space close to campus.

This Zen thing, though, was not Tibetan-style *anything*. Sure, there was a Buddha statue on an altar, but Tibetan-style altars have lots of water-offering bowls, lots of lights, lots of pictures, flowers, incense, rice, and fruit. This Korean-style Zen altar was just the Buddha, one water-offering bowl, two candles, and an incense burner. And when we sat it was in orderly rows, very still, and we all wore gray robes. Everyone! When I had sat with other groups, both in Nepal and in America, there had been a lot of fidgeting and shifting. But I tried to stick with it, even though I was attached to my Tibetan-style training.

Over the course of a semester, I decided that this Korean-style Zen thing was okay. The sitting and the chanting were helpful. The abbot of the Center, Bruce Blair, suggested I stay overnight and get up and do morning practice with everyone the next day. Morning practice was a little longer than evening practice and began at 5:00 A.M. with one hundred and eight bows.

I distinctly remember that first morning practice I attended at the New Haven Zen Center. I was used to the Tibetan style of bowing. I was also used to Tibetan leniency, where each person bows at his or her own pace. Not so at the Zen Center. "Together action," where everyone supports each other by acting together, means that bows are done in sync with each student in the dharma room matching his or her movements and pace to that of the head dharma teacher. I was busy bowing at my own pace and in my own style when the abbot kindly reminded everyone in the room that bows were to be coordinated. I immediately blushed, because I quickly realized that I was the one not doing "together action." I started bowing with everyone, but I had lost count of my bows. When the final bow came, it took me by complete surprise, and I blushed again. With everyone else moving in smooth, silent accord, my fumbling movements were obvious.

Perhaps most surprising to me was how *hard* Zen-style bowing was. My legs ached, and I couldn't walk down stairs or lower myself into a chair without wincing for days after my first set of morning bows. It's not that Tibetan-style bowing was easy, but I could use more of my whole body and compensate for weakness in my legs by pushing up with my arms. To do a Zen-style bow correctly, however, I had to lift my whole body up with my legs. I was sore.

I was also hooked on Zen. I still had a lot of questions about whether I should be practicing the Tibetan meditations I had begun with, or whether I should commit myself to Zen. I knew that consistency mattered in practice, and that mixing styles over time wouldn't be helpful. At that point, however, I thought: Zen. I'll do Zen. The Center was in my city, I really liked the community, and having a consistent practice was important and I could develop one at the Zen Center.

I also decided I wanted to move into the Center and become part of the residence program. I knew that being in residence would require a lot of discipline on my part, because each resident is required to go to a certain number of practice sessions per week and attend at least part of morning practice most days of the week. I was a senior in college by that time, and I had my senior essays to write, time to spend with my friends before we parted, and a part-time job on top of it all. But my practice was really important to me, and I knew that I needed a supportive living environment to keep my practice steady and constant.

I quickly discovered that, despite the early hour at which practice began and my typical half-awake state, starting off my day with practice changed my approach to the day. I felt ready and grounded when I began my day with practice. When I didn't give myself a chance to literally wake up with my practice in the morning and just rolled from bed to shower and out the door, I wasn't really awake for anything in my day, and not just in a physical sense. I wasn't as *present* for the people and situations I encountered. Practice in the morning helped me meet people and work with situations in a clearer, more direct way. And practice always began with bows.

Daily practice is important to develop discipline and help us day to day. All traditions have specific prayers and practices with which to begin the day. Often, especially in the cases of Judaism and Islam, morning prayers are a mandated part of orthodox practice. Even if we have a daily practice, however, all traditions recognize that intensive practice is also useful for our spiritual development. Muslims, for example, celebrate Ramadan, the month of fasting, or go on the hajj (pilgrimage), as times of concentrated contemplation and practice. All Buddhist schools also hold retreats, times when we can really focus on our practice and work with our minds. Retreats can be for only a day or as long as three years, although the latter are usually undertaken by monastics whose situation allows them to take that kind of time. In the Korean tradition, two three-month retreats are held each year, called Kyol Che, or "tight dharma." People can come and sit one week of the Kyol Che at a time, and though there are people each year who can take the full three months off from work, most of us can only do a week or two. I had sat a few weekend retreats, or *yong mae jong jin* ("to leap like a tiger while sitting"), and I thought, "Oh, I'll go do a week of Kyol Che for my spring break." Many people had talked about the benefits of sitting for at least a week, and the openness that could result from a longer retreat.

The Kyol Che was held at the head temple in Providence, Rhode Island. The Providence Zen Center has a small monastery on its grounds called Diamond Hill. Kyol Che was held there. I arrived the evening before I was supposed to enter the retreat and spent the night at the Providence Zen Center. The next morning, the three other people who were entering Kyol Che and I met and walked up to the monastery. It was in early March, and the sky was heavy and gray. The woods surrounding the Center and the monastery were severe, still a week or two away from spring buds, and the ground was frozen. We dropped off our bags in our rooms, went to a talk, and then Kyol Che for each of us began.

Having sat a retreat for no more than about a day and a half, I was intimidated by Kyol Che. It was almost three times longer than my longest retreat, with nine hours of *zazen* each day; about three hours of chanting Zen; three formal (silent) meals; and, of course, one hundred and eight bows every morning. At regular intervals, about every other day, each student would also have an interview with one of the two teachers who were leading the retreat.

I didn't start to get *truly* bored for about two days. I got a little bored, but I was also enamored of the idea of being on a Zen retreat. I was thinking, "Oh, I'm so cool. I'm sitting here at a monastery with Zen masters, monks, and other students. I'm cool. I'm a good Zen student."

This attitude holds up only until you realize that what you're doing is boring. The retreat was just sitting, just walking, just chanting, eating, and working during work period. No one talked, except in interviews, and those weren't time to chitchat. None of my friends could see how cool I was. They were in Peru, or Mexico, or Europe. They were drinking, partying, and seeing the world. What was I doing? Getting more and more stiff every hour that I sat, getting more and more bored every moment I didn't have a great realization, getting more and more discouraged each time I went into an interview and answered a *kong-an*—a kind of Zen riddle meant to cut off our thinking minds—but didn't attain the *kong-an*.

One of my main difficulties was my body. My back wasn't strong enough to sit for more than two days in a row. My knees weren't flexible either, and they hurt me. I was restless and in physical discomfort. I thought, "I can't make it. How do people do this for months?" In addition to my body complaining, my mind was racing, all the time. I thought about my senior essay, I concocted elaborate fantasies about situations and people, I imagined the taste of cheese pizza and red wine and longed for a huge slice of chocolate cake.

I decided to do bows to relieve my physical stiffness and to give myself something to do in my spare time. I also quickly realized that bowing is just bowing, and just as boring as sitting. I have to admit that I'm still working on "just being bored." It's hard just to be bored and not want to find a distraction! But at least when I bowed, my body was moving. I also found that bowing helped my mind calm down. The almost frantic leaping from one thought to another, and my difficulty in just letting all the thinking go, quieted a little with the regular rhythm and the hard work of bowing.

Zen Master Seung Hyang (Bobby Rhodes), my teacher, often says that we need to get down into our gut and act from there. This means we think too much. We're always in our heads. When we let go of thinking, we don't float away to someplace else, to a celestial plane or realm. We just settle into ourselves. We get down into our gut. We say all the time, "I had a gut feeling about that," or "My gut reaction is . . . " We already recognize with our speech that there is a different place from which we can react, instead of from our analytical mind. When we live from our gut, we aren't attached to our ideas about the way our lives should be. We are just living, responding with great openness and compassion to the situations that we encounter. This is enlightenment, just living, just waking up to every moment and not clinging to the moment. Bobby Rhodes also points out that when we bow, we bend from our middle, right where our gut is. Bowing helps us connect with this primary point, and get out of our heads and act without attachment.

I made it through my week of Kyol Che. Practice is strange, because when we're in it we're thinking, "This is too boring, this is too painful. I don't want to be here. I have better things to do." And then we finish our sitting or leave our retreat, and we see things a little more clearly, we feel less crazy and more open. I always think, "Ah! This practice thing, it really works." So I sign up for the next retreat or I get up in the morning, even when I don't want to go or get up for practice. Going or getting up even when I don't want to is a way to let go of my thoughts and emotions. Likes and dislikes are attachments. Wanting to do something or not wanting to do something are attachments to ideas about the way things should or shouldn't be. But we can't control everything, so we get upset when things don't turn out the way we wanted. When I get up in the morning, even when I don't want to, I'm trying to let go of my desire to achieve enlightenment without having to work for it—and especially my desire not to get up at five in the morning.

When we bow, we can just put down our likes and dislikes. Every morning, even if I oversleep and don't have time for all one hundred and eight bows, I try to do at least some bows. It's an important way to begin the day. Because I practice this thing called Zen Buddhism, I also say the Four Great Vows, which help me find my direction each day. One of the Four Vows is "Sentient beings are numberless, we vow to save them all." This is a Bodhisattva vow, because we are saying we will put down our selfish "small I," and attain our "big I." On the way to the floor as I bow, I try and put down my "small I." When my hands are palm up to the universe, I'm open to the sound of the birds outside, the neighbor getting his paper, the pipes in the house banging. I'm open to the moment and to my "big I." When I stand up, I'm more open, more compassionate—for at least a moment, until the next thought comes up and I chase it.

But if you really want to know what bowing is, then you have to do it.

BUDDHISM AND BOWING

Buddhism from pre-modern times was practiced as far west as present-day Afghanistan, and it is still practiced in the Far East, in China, Japan, and Korea. Now, Buddhism has come to America as well. Because Buddhism originated in Asian cultures, and a lot of different cultures at that, it's easy to think of the practice forms used in Buddhism as "Asian," "Chinese," "Tibetan," or "Korean." After all, Americans don't bow the way people do in Asian cultures. We shake hands. We don't sit cross-legged on mats; we sit in chairs. Judaism and Christianity have specific rules about not adoring idols, so many people who grew up in a Western culture don't like bowing to the Buddha statue on the altar because it goes against what they grew up being told about religious form.

Buddhism, however, is adaptable. American Buddhism is still emerging as we work with the forms our teachers brought with them from Sri Lanka, Tibet, China, Vietnam, Cambodia, Japan, Korea, and every other part of the world from which our teachers came. The practices in Buddhism have been around for more than twenty-five hundred years, so getting rid of bowing as a practice just because Americans and Westerners don't bow as they do in the East doesn't make sense. Rather, it's important for everyone, Buddhists and non-Buddhists alike, to understand how bowing (and other practice forms) helps us become aware of our minds and wake up to our true enlightened nature.

I practice Korean Zen Buddhism. So, as a way of providing a window into Buddhist history and practice in general, I will give a brief history of Zen Buddhism and then explore bowing in the Korean Zen tradition. Buddhism has a rich philosophical tradition and a broad history. The particulars of practice in each Buddhist tradition are also fascinating and have their own histories, which space does not allow me to investigate in great detail here. I encourage anyone who is interested in Buddhism to find a local temple or a sitting group to be able to taste Buddhism as a practice. Words have never been enough to explain any spiritual tradition. Engaging in it is the best way to understand a tradition or a practice. Nonetheless, I hope that this short introduction to Zen and bowing in Zen is helpful for exploring bowing as a spiritual practice.

ZEN BUDDHISM: WHERE IT CAME FROM, WHERE IT'S GOING

Once, sometime around the fifth century B.C.E., the Buddha Sakyamuni was giving a teaching at Rajagriha Mountain, which is in present-day India. He sat before the assembly of monks, nuns, and laypeople and said nothing for many minutes. Finally, he held up a flower—and only one monk, Mahakasyapa, understood his meaning and smiled. The Buddha said to Mahakasyapa, "I give you my true dharma."

This story about the origins of Zen illustrates one of the

most distinguishing features of Zen practice. The transmission of knowledge from teacher to student is a special mind-to-mind transmission, outside the scriptures that are usually the basis for testing knowledge and understanding in other Buddhist schools. When the Buddha held up the flower before the assembly, no one understood what he meant by the flower. But Mahakasyapa understood, and his smile showed that understanding. The Buddha, seeing Mahakasyapa's smile, knew that the monk had attained complete, one hundred percent awakening in the moment. Mahakasyapa had no confusion, no "What is going on here? What does the Buddha want? How can I be clever? Should I say anything?" Mahakasyapa put down all these busy thoughts, and just smiled. And that's enlightenment in Zen: just being awake and in the moment. Of course, even though Zen relies on a special transmission outside the scriptures, Zen still has its foundations and history in the philosophy and events shared by all Buddhist schools.

Zen is one school of Buddhist thought and practice. All Buddhist traditions share a common founder, the Buddha, Siddhartha Gautama, who was born approximately twenty-five hundred years ago, in the sixth century B.C.E., in what is now Nepal. *Buddha* means "the awakened one" in Sanskrit. After his awakening, or enlightenment, the Buddha taught for forty-five years until his death, and he founded a community of monks, nuns, and laypeople who continued to practice and study his teachings after his death. Over time, different schools of thought emerged. The three main branches of Buddhism are the Theravadan ("School of the Elders"), Mahayana ("Great Vehicle," of which Zen is one school), and Vajrayana ("Diamond Vehicle," also known as Tibetan Buddhism, although there are Vajrayana sects in Japan as well).

The Buddha's teachings and his awakening had two main points that distinguished him from other philosophers and teachers during his time. First, the Buddha taught the Four

Noble Truths. In brief, these are truths about suffering, the cause of suffering, the cessation of suffering, and the path to that cessation. The Buddha defined "suffering" as birth, old age, sickness, and death, as well as sorrow, grief, lamentation, and pain. From the moment we are born, we are moving toward the loss of our youth and our health, and our death comes closer. We must also face the loss of things and people we love, and we must face the things we do not like but cannot avoid. Our suffering comes from our attachments. We want some things and do not want other things, but we can't control everything that comes into or goes out of our lives. However, it's possible to let go of our attachments, and when we let go of our attachments, our suffering ceases and we "wake up," or attain enlightenment. To help us let go, we can follow the Noble Eight-Fold Path (right view, right thought, right speech, right action, right livelihood, right effort, right mindfulness, and right concentration).

Second, the Buddha taught that the "soul" is not actually a solid thing and has no identity in and of itself. The Buddha observed that all things change, arising in dependence upon causes and passing away when the causes also pass, and the soul or self is no different. The idea of a permanent soul was present in the pre-Hindu philosophy of the Buddha's time. The Buddha, however, taught that our soul, or sense of "I," does not exist as a permanent, unchanging, and substantive thing. This is the doctrine of *anatman* (Sanskrit, meaning "no-self" or "no-soul"). *Anatman* does not mean that an individual does not function— *anatman* is not nihilistic. Rather, our sense of self depends on the interaction of various aspects of our personality: our body, feelings, perceptions, actions, and consciousness. Even these depend on other causes. We could continue to break down the components of any seemingly permanent thing, such as an atom divided into electrons and protons, then subatomic particles, and so on. But the "atom" still works as an atom, even though there is no "atom" that is a single unit, without other components. Our "self" is like this atom, but we have a mistaken belief that our self is permanent. However, if we ask ourselves, deeply and with concentration, "What am I?" the answer comes back, "Don't know." All the components of our identity come together to make our sense of "I," and even though we could dissect our personality ad infinitum—really, we don't know what makes up this "I." Resting with this "don't know," just allowing ourselves to let go of all our preconceptions about identity and all of our desire to figure out who we are, is waking up.

All contemporary schools of Buddhism have their philosophical foundation in these two main points of the Buddha's teachings. "Zen" refers to several schools of Mahayana Buddhism that originated in China and then spread to and developed in Japan, Korea, and Vietnam. Buddhism first came to China in the first century C.E., and the focus of early Chinese Buddhism was on the translation and study of the sutras (discourses or scriptures) of Indian Buddhism. In the fifth century C.E., an Indian monk and meditation master named Bodhidharma came to China, and it is Bodhidharma whom Zen history considers to be the founder and first Chinese patriarch of Zen.

Zen was unlike the scholarly Buddhism that had prevailed in China since the first century. Bodhidharma said four things about Zen that help illuminate the heart of Zen practice:

> A special transmission outside the scriptures,
> Not dependent on words and letters;
> Direct pointing at the heart of man,
> Seeing into one's nature, one attains Buddhahood.

Zen taught that awakening was something outside the sutras and outside language in general. Studying the words of the sutras could not help us attain enlightenment. Only perceiving our true nature through direct insight would lead to enlightenment. The way to perceive our true nature is by keeping our mind one hundred percent focused and letting go of discursive thoughts. When we correctly perceive our own nature, then we have attained enlightenment.

All beings, not just humans, are able to wake up. Traditional Buddhist thought says that we are part of an endless cycle, called samsara, of birth, suffering, and death, only to be born again. Depending on whether or not we have hurt other beings or helped other beings, we take rebirth in various realms. If we have been helpful, or good, we are reborn as humans or in a heaven realm. If we have hurt others, then we are reborn as animals or in a hell realm. Waking up breaks this cycle of suffering. In a past life, we may have been an animal, or a ghost, or a kind spirit in Heaven. All beings—humans, animals, ghosts, and spirits—have Buddha-nature. Being human is ideal for practicing the path to enlightenment, and our precious rebirth as humans means that we should take this opportunity to wake up.

Zen Buddhism is immediate. Buddha and enlightenment aren't faraway states or events in the future. We have the ability and the opportunity to wake up right here, right now, to see the blue sky and green grass. We may practice for years and years without attaining enlightenment, and then suddenly, one day: Boom! Our minds open, our hearts open, we attain our true nature and see things as they really are.

Enlightenment isn't a special state. Really, enlightenment is ordinary. It's so ordinary we get bored; we make up all sorts of stories about our life and ourselves. We get attached to things, and we keep hanging on to them even when the situation or feeling changes and we get hurt. We have to put down all our expectations and all our desire for things to be a certain way. We just have to be with our everyday experiences.

Buddhism is just a way to label the path taught by the Buddha that leads to waking up. The truths that Buddhism points to about the human condition are not the special province of Buddhism alone, just as faith in God does not belong to only Jews, Christians, or Muslims. Only the particulars of practice and the vocabulary used by Buddhists are different from the paths and words taught by other great religious teachers throughout history.

All Buddhists practice meditation and study the sutras, although different schools use different collections of sutras. A qualified teacher in Buddhism has received transmission in an unbroken lineage from the time of the Buddha and has had his or her attainments recognized in a formal way by his or her teacher. Different schools of Buddhism also have different devotional practices to the Buddha, although all Buddhists make symbolic offerings to the Three Jewels, that is, the Buddha (teacher), Dharma (teachings), and Sangha (community). Buddhism also has a great variety of meditation practices, from the *metta* (loving-kindness) meditations in the Theravadan tradition, to the *shikintaza* ("just sitting") of Zen, to the mandala ("universe") visualizations of Vajrayana Buddhism. All these practices are meant as guides to help us on our way to waking up.

Many Buddhist schools and lineages have established themselves here in America. We now have the unique opportunity to study with many teachers from the various schools of Buddhist thought and practice. Sometimes this makes Buddhism less clear than if we had only one teacher and one practice to follow. Because *practice* is important—meaning consistent effort over time—leaping from one practice to another is more hindering than it is beneficial. When we begin to work with our minds, we should work hard, keep asking ourselves the question, "What am I?", and just be patient and put down our selfishness so we can help save all beings and wake up.

BOWING IN ZEN BUDDHISM

Bowing in Buddhism, and especially in Zen, is unique compared to bowing in other traditions. Bowing, rather than being an aspect of another practice such as prayer or reverence, *is* a practice in Buddhism. Bowing, done with single-minded focus, is meditation in motion. Although there are specific times when we should bow, such as when we enter or leave the meditation hall, when we greet a teacher, monk, or nun, and at certain times during the liturgy, the heart of bowing in Buddhism is putting our hands together, bowing deeply, and letting go of our small, selfish minds. Just like this: that's all bowing is.

Of course, bowing looks different from tradition to tradition. Because Buddhism spread all over the world and came into contact with many different cultures, each culture took some forms from Buddhism and then adapted them. My teacher, Zen Master Seung Sahn, came from Korea. He brought with him Korean-style bowing, and so his American students adopted this style and also worked with it so that this Korean-style bowing is also American-style bowing. The same has happened in va-

rious Tibetan Buddhist and Theravadan communities. For example, in the Shambhala teaching tradition, founded by Chögyam Trungpa Rinpoche, students don't even put their hands together in *anjali,* or prayer position; they just put their hands on their upper legs and bend from the waist.

Zen places an emphasis on constant awareness of what we are doing.

We attain enlightenment by paying one hundred percent attention all the time, so being mindful of our motions and our actions is a deep and central practice in Zen. Therefore, knowing the correct way to bow means being mindful at all times during the bow. Japanese Zen, especially the Rinzai School, is much more strict in their forms in general, including bowing. The way we hold our hands, the angle at which we incline our bodies, how deeply we should bow, and when, are all precisely performed in Rinzai Zen. Fortunately for me, and for other students of Dae Soen Sa Nim, Korean Zen is not as strict, although knowing how Korean Zen students bow certainly gives you a good idea of how other Zen schools bow, too.

There are two main forms of bowing, the half, or standing, bow and the full prostration. When we do a standing bow, we begin by standing upright, not stiffly but strongly, our spine in good alignment and our feet firmly placed on the floor, near one another. We should have a sense of physical grounding and strength whenever we do anything, especially in the meditation room and during practice. When we sit, walk, or bow, we should have good balance and posture. This helps us stay mindful, and it helps our bodies stay alert. So the standing bow has a sense of balance and strength in it.

Our hands should be in *anjali,* or *hapchang* in Korean, at our hearts. Dae Soen Sa Nim says that we should keep our palms pressed firmly, though not hard, together. This also helps us stay aware, because it requires a little effort to keep our palms together, so we are aware of the feeling in our hands. To begin the bow, we keep our backs straight and begin to bend from the waist. Our hands come down, still in *hapchang,* until we make a right angle with our backs and legs and our upper arms and forearms, our hands against our legs. My teacher, Zen Master Bobby Rhodes, says a bow is not complete until the muscles of your neck relax, because that's when you let go of pride and thinking. So our necks should also relax a little, but not so much that our heads are flopping all over! A standing bow is used to greet a teacher or show respect for the meditation hall where people are working to attain enlightenment, so we don't want to look sloppy or lazy.

A full prostration is used for showing respect to the teacher in formal situations, such as before practice in the meditation hall or in a one-on-one *kong-an* interview. Zen students also do one hundred and eight full prostrations each morning as a part of daily practice. A full prostration begins by standing with our hands in *hapchang,* just as in a standing bow. Instead of bending from the waist, however, we begin the bow by smoothly dropping our knees to our meditation mats. Then we put our hands, palms down, on the mat in front of us and place our left foot over our right. Then, at the same time, we turn our palms up, lean forward to put our foreheads on our mats, and lower our backsides to really stretch our bodies close to the ground. In Japanese Zen, we would then raise our palms to the height of our ears, which symbolizes our deep respect for the Buddha. In Asian countries, to touch our head to someone's feet is to show we consider them to be "higher" then we are, perhaps of great nobility or spiritual learning. In the American Korean Zen tradition I learned that the raising of hands is not done. Instead, we pause a moment with our foreheads on our mats and our hands open to the sky, then flex our feet to get ready to stand up and rock back onto our heels. We bring our hands back into *hapchang,* and then rise smoothly, using our legs to stand up straight.

The full prostration isn't always easy to do. I lose my balance frequently when I'm trying to stand up, and my legs get tired, especially during the one hundred and eight bows. But by paying attention to the motion, we can achieve a stillness of mind. When we put our hands out in front of us, our forehead down and our palms up, we are giving ourselves a physical example of how to train our minds: put down our ego, and open ourselves to the truth of our experience. When we show respect to the teacher and the Buddha in the meditation hall with our bows and prostrations, we are also showing respect to ourselves and to our own ability to attain enlightenment. We are the Buddha; we're just too busy and confused, with all our emotions and thoughts going a million miles an hour, to find our own Buddha-nature. So we bow to the teacher and the Buddha to show that we respect and will cultivate our own Buddha-nature.

Bows are usually done in sets of one, three, or one hundred and eight. Three is an auspicious number in Buddhism, as is one hundred and eight. I've heard various explanations for why one hundred and eight is significant—that humans have that many mental defilements, that the Buddha has that many names—but basically, I think that one hundred and eight is just enough bows to do without being too many for one set!

When we bow, if we have difficulty keeping our minds focused, we can use a mantra (a string of syllables connected to a certain idea or aspiration) to help focus our minds. The most

common mantra in my school of Zen is *Kwan Seum Bosal.* Literally, *Kwan Seum Bosal* means "perceive world sound" or "perceive world suffering." *Kwan Seum Bosal* is the Korean name for Avalokitesvara, the great Bodhisattva of Compassion. By repeating *Kwan Seum Bosal,* or the six-syllable mantra of Avalokitesvara, *Om Mani Padme Hum*—"All hail the Jewel in the Lotus (who is Avalokitesvara)"—we not only use a tool to focus our minds, but we also remind ourselves with every repetition of our motivation for bowing and for working toward enlightenment: to help other beings and to end suffering in the world.

We can use mantras when bowing, but the most important part of bowing is actually doing it with great mindfulness. Without mindfulness, bowing is an empty gesture, without benefit to our minds or practice. Whether we speak our intentions aloud, recite mantras to hold our aspirations to great compassion and wisdom close by, or say nothing at all matters less than letting go of our attachments and waking up. We can wake up without bowing, but the physical nature of bowing can be like little nudges. We say we let go of pride, or that we have open hearts, but if little (or big!) attachments remain, then bowing can nudge them loose and allow us to let go of our attachments even more.

One of the interesting aspects of Buddhism is that many people continue to practice their first spiritual tradition, such as Judaism or Christianity, while using the forms of Buddhism to help them still their minds and awaken their hearts. More and more often, teachers are holding Christian-Buddhist or Jewish-Buddhist retreats. The practices in Buddhism give us something we can do every day to help us be compassionate and wise, even if we aren't "Buddhist" but are Jewish, or Muslim, or none of the major world traditions. A teacher of mine, a Tibetan monk named Geshe Tashi, once said, "The Bible tells us, 'Love thy neighbor as thyself,' and Buddhism tells you how to do it!" I think he's right in that Buddhism, even though it's often called a religion, is actually a *path* with specific practices that help us to wake up. Bowing is certainly a practice that can benefit people from many different spiritual backgrounds, and what Buddhism teaches about how to bow can be taken to any synagogue, temple, mosque, church, or home and used to help us open our hearts and minds.

BOWING IN CHRISTIANITY, JUDAISM, AND ISLAM

The birth of the major world religions happened in remark-ably small and concentrated geographical areas. Perhaps this is the reason why we find greater similarity at the root of reli-gious thought, history, and ritual forms than we often assume, given the difficult and fractious relationships among different faiths in much of the world. But we should remember that Christianity, Judaism, and Islam all share not only a common geographical location, the Middle East, but cultural and political history as well. Similarly, Buddhism and Hinduism, discussed in the next chapter, both began on the Indian subcontinent, and both grew out of the Vedic philosophers of ancient India.

Yet another aspect of religious history we should keep in mind is that boundaries between cultures and religions have never been as static as history might make them seem. For example, when Buddhists living in what is now Afghanistan encountered Greek traders, they absorbed Greek artistic ideals. Prior to the interaction between these two very different cultures and religions, Buddhists had resisted representing the Buddha in human form. But after contact with Greek statuary, art, and principles of proportion, Buddhists adopted Greek art to represent the Buddha. The result was the face of the Buddha as we now know it.

In our exploration of our respective spiritual traditions, we should remember the sharing that has occurred since time immemorial. Somewhere in the past, one tradition grew from or with another tradition. I am not trying to dispense with doctrinal differences among religions, because these are central to each tradition, and they have profound effects on the practice of their followers. I am hoping, however, to encourage everyone to be open and willing to understand commonalities among traditions. With this hope in mind, I will give brief explanations of bowing in Christianity, Judaism, and Islam, and in the following chapter I will discuss Hinduism.

BOWING IN CHRISTIANITY: EASTERN ORTHODOX AND ROMAN CATHOLIC CHURCHES

In the Eastern Orthodox and Roman Catholic Churches, bowing has several different forms, used at specific times depending on the purpose of the bow. Protestantism, which usually lacks many of the ornate and highly ritualized aspects of worship found in the other two branches of Christianity, has moments of reflection and prayer during which people bow their heads or the congregation kneels together. Protestants do not, however, all share the same exact physical practices. I have chosen to look most closely at Eastern Orthodox and Roman Catholic bowing practices because the formality and ritual of bowing in these traditions is well defined and commonly practiced.

In Eastern Orthodox practice, the two major forms of bowing are called the small *metania* and the grand *metania*. *Metania* is a Greek word meaning "to turn" or "to change," and it connotes a turning or changing of our internal state. In Christianity, the turning is away from sin and toward God, and in the New Testament, which is written in Greek, *metania* is the word used for repentance.

The small *metania* is most often used during the liturgy. We make the small *metania* with our right hand, placing the thumb, pointer, and middle fingers together and laying the ring and pinkie finger against the palm. The three fingers together represent the tri-unity of God, and the two fingers against the palm represent the dual nature of Christ as both human and Divine. We make the Sign of the Cross over our bodies, using the right hand and the three fingers placed together to draw the cross on our bodies. We place the fingers first at our forehead, then at our navel, then at the right shoulder, and lastly at the left—although in Roman Catholicism the Sign of the Cross is made by touching the fingers first to the left shoulder and then to the right. After making the Sign of the Cross, we bow deeply from the waist and touch the ground with our right hand. In the Slavic Eastern Orthodox Churches, the Sign of the Cross comes after we touch the ground, but the components of the small *metania* (crossing ourselves and touching the ground) are present in all the various Eastern Orthodox congregations.

The grand *metania* is a full prostration. We put our knees and our hands on the ground and bring our forehead to touch

the earth, and then rise again. The grand *metania* is most often performed upon entering a church and before highly respected people, such as a bishop. Bowing, a simple inclination of the head, is also used in Eastern Orthodoxy, but it is less formal than either the small or the grand *metania,* and it is usually reserved for less ritualized adoration or homage to a person or an icon.

In the Roman Catholic Church, bowing, genuflecting, kneeling, and prostrating are all used in the course of worship. Bowing, as in the Eastern Orthodox Church, is an inclination of the head used to show respect and homage, but is used in a less formal way than other forms of bowing. Bowing and its various forms in the Roman Catholic tradition came from the same concept of *metania,* "to turn oneself around," that the Eastern Orthodox tradition uses. Even though the names of the forms and the forms themselves are different in the two traditions, the purpose behind them is the same. Considering that the two churches were once a universal, single body of worship and belief, this is not surprising.

Genuflection, in which either one knee (the right) or both knees are dropped to the ground, occurs at two times during Catholic worship. When the bread and wine of the Eucharist (the bread and wine that become the body and blood of Jesus Christ) are consecrated during the Mass, the congregation genuflects with both knees on the ground and bows their heads. When entering or leaving the church, however, genuflecting on one knee in the direction of the altar holding the Eucharist is sufficient. Usually the Sign of the Cross is performed at the same time as the genuflection.

Full prostrations, which involve placing the entire body on the ground before the altar, are performed as part of the service only by the clergy, usually when taking ordination as a monk, nun, or priest. The practice of prostration actually came from Asian countries and was adopted by Christians as a way to show great respect to the Divine. Similarly, genuflection came from secular European society, in which vassals bent their knee before their liege lord. Gradually, this act of respect was incorporated into the celebration of the Mass in the Catholic tradition—it's not found in the Orthodox tradition because genuflection came from Western European traditions. The external form came from secular society, but the commandment to show physical respect to God goes back to the Bible. In Philippians 2:10, it is written, "at the name of Jesus every knee should bend, in Heaven and on earth and under the earth." This passage gives the various forms used in Christianity a scriptural foundation.

Kneeling originally was used for private prayer alone; later, prayers in the liturgy used during congregational worship that were penitent in nature or were considered to be part of an individual's personal (private) preparation were said while kneeling. Genuflection on both knees is similar in appearance to kneeling, but it occurs at different times during the worship and liturgy. Genuflection is a sign of respect, and kneeling is a sign of penitence before God.

All of these external actions are meant to join with the interior turning or changing of our attitude from sin to God. If genuflection and *metania,* small or grand, are not accompanied by our own inner resolution to change our habits and enrich our compassion and relationship with God, then all the outer manifestations of faith and repentance mean nothing. They are empty ritual, and sacrilegious. Baptism, which is the ritual that signifies entrance into the Christian family and the redemption of the baptized individual's soul in Christ, is the first turning away from sin that Christians take. In a simple and small way, the turning away from sin symbolized by all the forms of bowing in Christianity is a renewal of baptism. Submission is also an aspect of Christian faith, in that we must submit to God's will. Bending our knees and lowering our heads before God shows not only respect and our desire to change our habits of mind that lead us into wrong actions, but also our submission to the will of God, that in profession of faith in Jesus we may be saved.

To bow is to partake in the hope and promise of redemption and forgiveness that Jesus brought to humanity, and to turn away from our smaller, selfish habits and toward the open and loving heart Jesus shared with the people of the world. Private prayer leaves more room for spontaneity, but coming together as a community to receive the Eucharist and praise God is an important part of Christian faith. The established forms of communal worship give us the opportunity to let go of concerns about what to do next. Instead, we can focus on bringing our whole heart and mind to God.

BOWING IN JUDAISM

Judaism is the oldest of the world's monotheistic religions, and it is from Jewish history that both Christianity and Islam emerged, each in its own way and with its own relationship to the history and characters who drive the stories of this ancient tradition and belief system. Modern Jews and Judaism are remarkable both in their deep connections to tradition and history and in their interpretation and reinterpretation of that tradition.

Although modern Jewish movements differ greatly in their views of the strictures that Halakhah (the body of Jewish law from Torah and from tradition) places on individuals, several constants hold across movements. One is that community and tradition are central to Jewish practice, even if adherence to traditional ritual observance and faith in God are not always present. Members of one movement can step into the synagogue of another movement and easily recognize the daily and yearly cycle of prayers in the services, because all Jewish congregations follow the same principles of community worship, historical commemoration, and tradition, although each movement interprets that tradition somewhat differently.

Orthodox and other ritually observant Jews pray three times daily, in the morning, midday, and evening, and also on the Sabbath (sundown Friday to sundown Saturday each week), either as part of a congregation or individually. Each service has specific prayers associated with it, but many of the prayers are constant from service to service. Additionally, for the ritually observant, when and how one stands, sits, and bows are regulated by tradition, and for other Jews they are guided by tradition. Liturgical prayer, and by extension bowing, is not a spontaneous event in Judaism. Rather, the ritual and rite of prayer provide a formal structure in which we are freed from worrying about what to do or say next, and we are able to more fully engage in what we are doing and saying in the moment.

Within the daily cycle of prayers, some prayers, such as the *Shemoneh Esrei,* or "The Eighteen [blessings]," specifically require bowing as part of the traditional recitation. The *Shemoneh Esrei* is also known as the *Amidah,* which means "standing," because the worshiper stands while reciting it. At the beginning of the *Amidah,* which is part of the liturgy in all Jewish services, tradition has the worshiper take three steps forward. These three steps signal entrance into God's presence, and at the end of the prayer the worshiper takes three steps backward to withdraw from God's presence. During the prayer itself, the worshiper bows several times. To bow, we bend our knees, then straighten and gently bend from the waist. These bows are performed at the points in the *Amidah* when God is praised. The *Amidah* is a petitionary prayer, and the bows are meant to remind the petitioner of God's sovereignty and his or her submission to that sovereignty. Some people may also move in a swaying back-and-forth motion during standing prayer. This motion is called *shuckling,* derived from Yiddish. A friend of mine, Rabbi Lina Grazier-Zarbarini, described *shuckling* as "throwing yourself into prayer," and so even though it is not a formal bow, *shuckling* serves a similar purpose to bowing in that it uses the body to engage us in prayer. Among some Orthodox Jews *shuckling* can be similar to repeated strenuous bowing from the waist during prayer.

Twice a year, at Rosh Hashanah and at Yom Kippur, the traditional Orthodox liturgy includes a full prostration. In most Orthodox congregations where this is done, only the person leading the service, usually the cantor or rabbi, performs the prostration as the prayer messenger of the community; in some ultra-Orthodox congregations, the entire community is invited to prostrate before God. While it is extremely rare for full prostration to be practiced in non-Orthodox congregations, for Rabbi Lina, these prostrations are important and precious times in her spiritual practice. "I love it," she says of the prostrations. "I find it a very powerful moment. I'm usually alone in front of everyone, humbling myself before God and the congregation. I feel like I never want to get up."

Because forms of worship draw from Torah as well as from rabbinic interpretation and cultural tradition, bowing in Judaism has both a biblical and a cultural history. The Hebrew Bible mentions in specific passages the act of falling down prostrate, kneeling, and bending the knees as forms of adoration or reverence. Prostration and bowing antedate even Judaism and have their roots in the pre-Judaic religions and customs of the ancient Middle East. As Judaism developed, it absorbed or rejected the physical customs of others in the Middle East. Lying prostrate on the ground, or prostrating when entering the Temple of ancient Judaism, arose both from scriptural descriptions of biblical figures and from the habitual attitude of reverence toward more worldly figures, such as kings. In worship, God, being the King of kings, was due more reverence, but the worshiper used a familiar physical act of submission. Gradually, the forms of bowing and prostration were codified and regularized in the Jewish community.

In Judaism, the relationship between God and humanity is one of partnership. We have an obligation to follow our better impulses, our *yetzer tov,* to continue the work of creation that God began and to end the suffering and strife in the world. The commandments, such as the commandment to pray and to "bend our knees and bow" before God, connect us to God and to God's work so that our work in this world is for good and for the good of humanity. Bowing, however, also reminds us that we are in submission to God and in need of God's help and blessing. Prayer and bowing remind us that humility is necessary for us to act for the benefit of all, and not just for the benefit of ourselves. According to Rabbi Lina, because humans are created in God's image, "there's some potential for lack of humility." But "because of the exalted nature of our creation, we have tremendous obligation. There are these physical things we do—like bowing and prostration—that remind us we are not the center of our own universe. Every prayer is a charge to go out there and fix the world. It's good to have physical practices that remind us that we have the obligation to be part of the process of creation; we are neither at the beginning nor at the end of that process."

BOWING IN ISLAM

Islam has five pillars of faith, which are the heart of Islamic belief and practice: the *shahadah* (profession of faith), *salat* (prayer), *sawm* (fasting during Ramadan), *zakat* (giving alms to the needy), and the *hajj* (pilgrimage to Mecca). The second pillar of faith is *salat,* or prayer. The word *salat* actually means prayer in both its internal and external forms, that is, both the words and attitudes of prayer and the physical actions of bowing and prostration that the Prophet Muhammad practiced and gave to his followers as the proper way to pray.

Salat is an exact and precise practice. The recitation of salutations, praises, *suras* (chapters) from the Qur'an, petitions, and aspirations all have specified and restricted places in *salat*. Likewise, what we do with our bodies during *salat* is specific and sensitive to where we are in the stage of a prayer.

The inner state that spoken prayer cultivates and the exterior postures that express the inner state are intimately linked in

Islam. Although submission to God's will is a part of both Judaism and Christianity, only in Islam is submission the major aspect of the relationship between God and humanity. The precepts that God gave humanity through the previous prophets such as Abraham and Elijah and, most important, through the Prophet Muhammad are laws, to which a Muslim must submit as well. Therefore, the way in which a Muslim performs *salat* is not determined by slow changes in culture over time, or by the absorption of practices from secular society. Muhammad practiced and passed on *salat* in detail to the Islamic community, and the form of practice comes straight from God through him.

Salat can be performed any time during the day except during sunrise and sunset, but *salat* is commanded at the five specific times of dawn, mid-morning, noon, mid-afternoon, and dusk. *Salat* can be performed anywhere, although the entire community should gather at a mosque for the Friday noon prayer. For both men and women, modest dress is important for prayer and attendance at a mosque. At a mosque, women and men worship in different areas—women often pray in a balcony, in a reserved space screened off from a main area, or behind the men—so that both men and women won't be distracted from prayer by the presence of the opposite sex. This is the same in Orthodox Judaism.

To prepare for *salat,* we first go through ablutions called *wadu,* or ritual washing. This not only cleanses the body, but also emphasizes the sacred nature of prayer and communication with God. After ablutions, we develop an intention behind our prayer. This intention is silent, something communicated less with words and more with our own willingness and gladness to take upon ourselves the practice of *salat* as commanded by God and performed by Muhammad. We form our intention as we physically approach the place designated for prayer, and we orient ourselves so that we face toward Mecca. In America, we face eastward to orient ourselves to Mecca. Every mosque has a niche in the wall, called a *qibla,* that locates the direction for prayer.

The first step of *salat* is the *takbeer,* in which we say, *"Allahu akbar"* (Allah is the greatest). When saying this, our hands come up to our ears, and when we have finished with the *takbeer,* our hands come down to our chest and the right hand grasps the left wrist. Next are the opening supplications and the recitation of the *suratul fatiha,* said with our hands over our chests and our eyes fixed down and in front of us. The supplications and the *suratul fatiha* ask for God's forgiveness and mercy and emphasize our faith in one God and our turning away from evil.

The *ruku',* or bowing, follows the opening announcement, supplication, and praise. We begin with another *takbeer,* our hands at our ears, then we bow with our backs straight and our hands open on our knees. While making *ruku',* we recite praise to God by saying, *"Subhana rabbi yal azim"* (How perfect is my Lord, the Supreme). After the *ruku',* we rise back to standing, saying, *"Sami' Allah hu liman hamidah, rab-bana wa lakal hamd"* (Allah listens to the one who praises Him, our Lord, to You be all praise).

Next is the *sujud* (prostration). We begin with the *takbeer* again; say, *"Allahu akbar,"* with our hands at our ears; and then we prostrate. Our knees touch the ground before our hands, which are spread open, palms facing down, and our forehead and nose both touch the ground. Our feet remain flexed against the ground, with only the toes touching. While going down into *sujud,* we recite *subhana rabbi yal a'la* three times. The seven points of the body touching the ground—the toes, knees, hands, and face—are the seven limbs that the Prophet Muhammad pressed to the ground during his prayers.

After the full prostration, we raise our head and say, *"Allahu akbar."* Then we rise into a sitting position, while keeping the right foot flexed and letting the left foot lie flat on the ground. Our hands rest on our knees, and we recite, *"Rabb ighfirlee wa irhamnee"* (O my Lord! Forgive me and have mercy on me). Then we repeat the *sujud* and the recitations. At the completion of all the recitations, we recite the closing blessings while looking first to our right (toward the angel recording our good deeds), and then to the left (toward the angel recording our bad deeds). Any personal prayers we have we recite while sitting back on our right foot, our hands cupped and palms up at chest level. Then we stand and greet those standing around us; the *salat* is complete.

Across all of the shared origins and history of the world's three major monotheistic traditions, bowing has a place in each tradition's ritual and worship. The physical act of submission and penitence—bowing, genuflection, kneeling, and prostration—are part of the richly beautiful relationship between each individual and the Divine. Bowing forms a bridge not only between the Christian, Jewish, and Islamic traditions, but also with Hinduism and Buddhism, the traditions that originated and developed on the Indian subcontinent. In the next chapter, we will continue our exploration of bowing in the Hindu tradition.

BOWING IN OTHER EASTERN TRADITIONS

BOWING IN HINDUISM

One of the basic ideas in Hinduism is the presence of the Divine in every being. Hinduism has, at first glance, a confusing and vast pantheon of gods, goddesses, and other divine beings. So which or what "divine" is present? This pantheon of gods and goddesses is considered to represent, in a variety of forms, the many aspects of human actions, personalities, and desires. In this sense, Hinduism is both polytheistic and monotheistic, because every deity and every being is a part and manifestation of the Ultimate Divine. The devotional and meditation practices in Hinduism are aimed at bringing us into accord with our own divine natures.

Bowing in Hinduism looks like, and functions in a similar manner to, bowing in Buddhism. This should not surprise us, because Buddhism emerged from Hindu religion and philosophy, and although it set itself somewhat in opposition to the Hindu thinkers of its time, Buddhism still incorporated many of its spiritual, metaphysical, and theological structures and practices. It can be easy to mistakenly substitute Buddhist ideas for Hindu ones, and vice versa, because the same words are used to describe major philosophical points. Karma, dharma, *moksha* (Sanskrit for "liberation"), and many other words form the vocabulary for both traditions. So when we explore bowing in Hinduism, even though it looks and sounds a lot like bowing in Buddhism, we need to understand Hinduism's ultimate goal, which is union with the Divine, rather than "enlightenment" as Buddhists understand it.

Understanding the *why* of bowing in Hinduism is important, because while there are certain situations when bowing is expected, bowing is rarely formalized the way it is in other world religions. Sometimes people perform a full prostration upon entering a temple; other times, people do not. It depends on what their personal practice is, and what spirit moves them at any given moment. Entering or exiting a temple, greeting elders and holy men and women, and performing *puja,* or ceremony, are the situations in which some form of bowing, from a simple inclination of the head with hands in *anjali* to a full prostration, is customary. But it is up to each individual to decide how to bow at these times, rather than follow a uniform or strict practice.

Swami Padmapadananda, a resident at Sivananda Yoga Ranch in Woodbourne, New York, explained to me that "to offer all of one's self in the form of devotion—including bowing and prostrating—is to manifest love and unity with the Divine, and also to bring together the 'external' body and the 'internal' spirit. But the reality is, everything is God. The Divine is the substratum for all of reality. A person is a manifestation of God, or the Divine, and all of existence is one absolute reality of pure spirit. To be able to realize this in all situations is the goal, to go beyond the external and the material." When we bow in Hinduism, we are honoring the Divine in ourselves and in others.

This honoring, as well as the important idea of unity between opposites (external/internal, Divine/human, and so on), forms the backbone of Hindu bowing. A mental bow is as important as a physical bow. Also, because of the diversity of practices, teachers, and ritual worship in Hinduism, no one form can be considered paramount to all others.

A Hindu priest, Swami Vasishtananda, at the Sivananda Yoga Ranch, also had great insight into the significance of the physical and external practice of bowing. One of the most common times when people bow to one another is in greeting, called *namaskar* or *namaste*. According to the swami, the word *namaskar* or *namaste*—which is popularly translated as "I salute the Divine in you"—originally came from two root words. One root, *nama,* means "not mine." When we bow, or perform *namaskar* (which happens most often in greeting, but really encompasses every time we bow), we are bowing to something we perceive as external, or "not mine." *Skaram,* the other root, means "salutation." The Swami said that one way to look at *namaskar* is not only as bowing to the Divine in others, but also as saying to ourselves, "When I bow to you, I surrender to the Lord, and it is not for selfish reasons. It is for *you.*" Part of our divine nature is innate compassion and love. Surrendering to the Divine is not so that we can glorify ourselves, saying, "Oh, I'm holy, I'm divine, I'm more special than anything—or anyone—else." This surrender is so that, through our innate, pure, divine nature, we can wake up our better selves and practice compassion, love, and wisdom to help those around us. We have to let go of our own agendas and our own ideas of what our nature is, or our ego obstructs our ability to see the Divine not only in ourselves, but also in others.

The form of bowing most commonly associated with *namaskar* is the universal greeting used by Hindus for teachers, holy places, friends, and strangers alike. The hands are placed in *anjali* at the heart or in front of the head, and the head may also be inclined. By bringing our hands together in *anjali,* we reflect upon the unity we can achieve by bringing separate elements together. Often, when the person being greeted is an elder or a teacher, the greeter may also bend down to touch his or her hands to the feet of the elder, to show the high esteem in which the greeter holds the other person. To place ourselves below another's feet, either literally or symbolically, shows that we are thankful and humble before those who command our respect.

Other forms of bowing in Hinduism include what we, as Westerners, may at first think of as a "yoga posture," the Sun Salutation postures, or *Surya Namaskar.* We should remember, however, that the word *yoga* means "unity," and that the practice of physical postures is meant to harmonize the body and the spirit, and bring them into unity with one another. The *Surya Namaskar* series of postures are meant not only to emphasize the unity between the body and soul, but also to offer worship to the Sun, a personified deity, and to underscore the fundamental divine nature of all creation.

The full prostration, with the entire body laid down "like a stick," or parallel to and on the ground, is also used in Hinduism. This form is usually restricted to men alone; it was not considered appropriate for women to bow in a similar way. All seven limbs—the legs, arms, body, and head—should touch the earth. Many sages use full prostration to complete long pilgrimages, much as Buddhists do. The Earth, like the Sun, is also a personified deity, and just as we can offer prostrations to the Sun, so may we also offer prostrations to the Earth and seek a greater unity with it by actually placing our entire bodies on the ground.

There are also times during Hindu rituals and ceremonies when bowing or prostration is called for, but the sheer number of rituals and ceremonies, and the differences from teacher to teacher, is so great that to catalog them would be difficult. We can generally say, however, that any time a sacred space or time is entered or departed, a bow or prostration is appropriate.

Hinduism's rich diversity of practices, rituals, devotions, and teachers finds unity in the Ultimate Divine, which permeates all beings. Bowing, in all its forms in Hinduism, allows us to "overcome the ego in a positive way, by seeing the Divine in yourself and others," as Swami Padmapadananda put it. From a simple greeting to an elaborate ritual, bowing in Hinduism is meant to cultivate oneness and selflessness. It is as much a mental action as a physical one.

As I hope is apparent from these brief explorations of bowing, every tradition has a rich history accompanying its forms of bowing. In all traditions, simply going through the motions isn't enough to bow truly. We must engage our entire selves in the mental and physical action of bowing. Whatever your own tradition, I hope you are inspired to look more closely at the history of bowing and at the relationship between spiritual thought and religious forms. Although the emphasis of our spiritual practice should be on *practice* and not on theory or history, if we combine practice with knowledge, we can often arrive at a deeper appreciation and understanding of what we do in our spiritual traditions and why we do it.

THREE THOUSAND BOWS FOR A QUESTION: STORIES THAT INSPIRE

Every religious and spiritual tradition has a history. These histories contain stories and characters that inspire us with their events, words, and deeds. Our stories convey the heart of spiritual practice and values from one generation to another, and the "history" of a tradition is always growing to include the present and immediate past. Stories also shape our contemporary impressions and ideas about our tradition. Bowing, for example, appears time and again in Buddhist stories as one of the practices of a sincere or accomplished practitioner. Masters and students, legendary figures and everyday people, practitioners from the distant past and practitioners from our own present have all used bowing as a mainstay of their practice. We don't have to be Buddhist, or practice Buddhism, to find inspiration in these stories. When we contemplate the commitment and hard work others have put into their practices, we can learn something from their dedication and put that lesson into action in our own practices.

With that in mind, I have collected a few stories from the Buddhist tradition that reflect the ubiquitous nature of bowing as a practice. First, I want to introduce some of the more legendary characters from Buddhist history, practitioners whose words and actions have served as examples for people throughout time. Second, I want to introduce a few people who are alive and practicing today. There are great Asian masters who practice in Manhattan, Americans who study in Seoul or Dharamasala, Zen centers in Poland, and Sri Lankan monks in Paris. All over the world, ancient traditions find new homes in other cities, and synagogues and churches have mosques and temples as neighbors. Contemporary practitioners are people just like us, and for this reason they are all the more inspiring.

I hope that you, like me, find these stories relevant to your spiritual practice, whether established, growing, or just beginning. One important thing to remember as we read these stories is that bowing always takes place within the larger structure of practice. It is less important that someone complete a certain number of prostrations, or bow from one place to another, and more important that he or she make a sincere effort to practice. Not many of us have the expanses of time that the great teachers had. But we can look at their great accomplishments and see the possibility for our own efforts and practice. We don't have to be special or highly realized to bow. We just have to do it one hundred percent. This is the core teaching in all these stories—that effort, sincerity, and concentration yield an open heart and mind.

ONE MILLION PROSTRATIONS: THE TIBETAN MASTER TSONGKHAPA

Tsongkhapa, also known as Je Rinpoche and Lobsang Drakpa, is one of the central figures in Tibetan Buddhist history. Born in 1357 in eastern Tibet, Tsongkhapa was recognized at an early age as a reincarnation of one of Buddha Sakyamuni's students. He took novice monk's vows at the age of seven, and by that age he had also received many central tantric (esoteric) teachings from eminent teachers of his day. He took full monk's vows when he was twenty-five years old. Tsongkhapa is most remembered for establishing the Gelugpa monastic tradition and lineage. The present Dalai Lama, although he studies in all four of the Tibetan lineages, is primarily schooled in the Gelugpa tradition. As a scholar, Tsongkhapa's ability not only to retain teachings but also to attain the heart of wisdom and compassion at the core of Buddhist thought earned him renown and respect from other scholars of his day.

Tsongkhapa, certainly one of the preeminent scholars of Tibetan Buddhism, was also a great practitioner. In addition to his years of study and teaching, he did many retreats, the longest of which was four years. During one particular retreat, Tsongkhapa performed over a million full-body prostrations as part of his purification practices. This purification, called *ngondro* (Sanskrit for "something which precedes"), is usually preparation for receiving certain high teachings in Tibetan Buddhism. The first practice of *ngondro* is prostrations. For a practitioner, these prostrations are "refuge prostrations," meaning that as one does the prostration, one recites a refuge prayer, taking refuge in the Buddha, Dharma, *Sangha,* one's teacher, and other spiritual guides. As part of *ngondro,* the practitioner must complete 111,111 prostrations—in addition to one million mantra recitations, 111,111 symbolic mandala (universe) offerings, and 111,111 visualizations! Tsongkhapa had already completed at least one *ngondro* cycle, and it's not unusual to do the entire *ngondro* practice several times over the course of one's practice. By the time he went on his four-year retreat, it is probable that he had already done several hundred thousand prostrations in the context of *ngondro,* not to mention the daily prostrations that are part of regular practice and ritual in Tibetan Buddhism. All together, he is said to have completed three and a half million prostrations during his lifetime.

Tsongkhapa, unlike many of us, was a monk who was able to use all his time, starting from when he was a young boy, to engage in formal practice. Although he had numerous responsibilities as a teacher, he was also able to do long retreats. His situation, that of a brilliant reincarnated monk in fourteenth-century Tibet, seems different from many of our situations and lives. But Tsongkhapa's story also teaches us about the power of commitment and determination. Many laypeople, both Tibetan and Western, give a portion of their life to practice. At holy sites throughout Tibet, Nepal, and India, you can see Tibetan practitioners doing full-length prostrations as part of their *ngondro* practice, especially on holidays. A three- or four-year retreat isn't always possible, but we can still follow Tsongkhapa's example and take some time out—a day, a weekend, a month, or whatever fits our life situations—and use that time to focus on our practice. Over a lifetime, we too can accomplish one million prostrations.

THREE STEPS, ONE BOW ACROSS CHINA: EMPTY CLOUD ZEN MASTER'S LEGACY

Zen Master Hsu-yun ("Empty Cloud") was born in China in 1840. Until his death in 1959, Hsu-yun worked tirelessly to live and teach according to the rich Chinese Buddhist tradition that he inherited. Like Tsongkhapa in Tibet, Hsu-yun was a multifaceted and skilled Buddhist teacher and practitioner. Chinese Buddhism had entered a period of decline when Hsu-yun became a monk. Monasteries were rife with corruption, temples had fallen into neglect and disrepair, and monastic discipline was almost entirely lacking. Through his sincere example and industrious efforts to rebuild key temples and monasteries, including the Temple of the Sixth Patriarch (the home of Hui-neng, whom contemporary Korean Zen considers to be its founder), Hsu-yun revitalized the study and practice of Buddhism for monastics and laypeople alike.

Among his most inspiring activities were his bowing pilgrimages to holy sites in China and the Indian subcontinent. Hsu-yun made his way from one place to another by taking three steps and one bow. A slow, difficult, and often painful way to travel, these bowing pilgrimages cultivated and emphasized the humility and faith of Hsu-yun. His longest pilgrimage, during which he visited Putuo Island (sacred to the Bodhisattva of Compassion) and Mount Wu-tai in Shansi (sacred to the Bodhisattva of Wisdom), took him three thousand miles across China over the course of six years. He also traveled to Tibet, Bhutan, Ceylon, and Burma before returning to China, always by taking three steps and one bow, across mountains and rivers.

Fifty years after Hsu-yun's journey, two American monks in the Chinese Buddhist tradition decided to follow Hsu-yun's example. In November 1973, Hung Ju and Hung Yo made a "three steps, one bow" pilgrimage up the coast of California. They journeyed more than one thousand miles in this way. Imagine walking out your front door, and bowing down the block! What would your neighbors think? Your family, or your friends? A bowing pilgrimage looks out of place in America, but these monks, inspired by the strength of Hsu-yun's practice, decided to bring an old practice form into a new context, and their story is proof that such traditions do not belong to the past alone, but are ours to claim and make our own.

FOURTEEN DAYS AROUND DRAGON MOUNTAIN: A CONTEMPORARY PRACTICE AND PILGRIMAGE

The Kwan Um School of Zen is an international school founded by a Korean monk, Zen Master Seung Sahn (also called Dae Soen Sa Nim). Dae Soen Sa Nim, like many of the teachers who founded Buddhist lineages here in the West, has inspired his students with his own practice. Although he grew up in a Protestant household in Korea, Dae Soen Sa Nim became disillusioned with the world when he was in his late teens and retreated to the mountains, determined to find the source of human suffering and sorrow. While in the mountains, he met at a local Buddhist temple a young monk, who gave him a Buddhist scripture to read. What Dae Soen Sa Nim read there changed him forever. Finding in the text an answer to his questions about suffering and reality, he went to the temple and became a novice monk.

After his novice training, he went into a cave on Duk Sahn Mountain to do a one-hundred-day retreat. On the last day of his retreat, as he was chanting, the sound of the *moktak* (a percussive instrument used to keep the beat during chanting) and his mind became one, and he woke up. After that retreat, he was called Zen Master Seung Sahn ("man of Duk Sahn Mountain"). He was only twenty-two.

Many stories about Dae Soen Sa Nim's sincere and strong practice abound in my school. One of my senior teachers, Zen Master Dae Kwang, told me that Dae Soen Sa Nim used to do five hundred bows before regular morning practice, every day. To me, the most telling proof of Dae Soen Sa Nim's own practice is the practice he has inspired in his students.

Like Hsu-yun in China, and Hung Ju and Hung Yo in California, two monks from the Kwan Um School (both of whom are American) decided to make a "three steps, one bow" pilgrimage around Kye Ryong San Mountain in Korea, considered a holy place. One of the monks, Myong Haeng Sunim ("Sunim," derived from Korean, is an honorific title used for both monks and nuns, similar to the Tibetan title "Rinpoche"), wrote about his experience in *Primary Point* magazine. I contacted Myong Haeng Sunim and asked him about his experiences, because unlike Zen Master Hsu-yun, Tsongkhapa, or even Dae Soen Sa Nim (who gets a lot of mail!), Myong Haeng Sunim was available to answer direct questions about bowing as a practice. What I received in return was a wonderfully open, generous and heartfelt story about one individual's life and spiritual path. Because I can't tell his story any better, I give it to you in his words. I was excited that I had the opportunity to ask someone alive and accessible about his practice, and I hope that you also feel Myong Haeng Sunim's energy and receive inspiration from his story.

My name is Myong Haeng Sunim, and I was born on September 26, 1970, in Madison, Wisconsin. I first became interested in spiritual practice while attending Cornell University in Ithaca, New York. In my last year at the university, I joined a Zen meditation group led by a local Ithaca teacher named David Radin, who had been a student of Suzuki Roshi. I began to focus my life on practice, joining simultaneously a Japanese Zen group, a Tibetan meditation group, and a tai chi class.

In June 1993, I made the decision to go to Korea and become an English teacher, mainly due to extensive debts I had accumulated during my time at Cornell, but also following some deep-rooted desire to live in Asia. Before I left Ithaca I asked my American Zen teacher if he knew of any Zen practice in Korea. He knew of only one Korean Zen Master, who had been teaching in America for many years and had many Western disciples. This turned out to be Zen Master Seung Sahn. But all my American Zen teacher could say about Korean Buddhism was that it involved a lot of bowing, which seemed horrifying to me at the time.

Most of my first two years as a layperson in Korea were spent drinking and carousing. I also tried to keep a personal practice by sitting every day by myself, even between classes at the language school. I visited a Korean Zen monk on one of my first days in Korea, but due to the language barrier and the early hour at which he required me to come to the temple, I was not able to really connect with him.

During this first year I lived in a small town called Chin-Ju, located about two hours west of Pusan. In 1994 I moved to a larger city named Daejeon, where I spent another year teaching. Within two years I had paid off all of my debts from Cornell, and I was faced with the basic question of what to do next with my life. I still had this strong idea to practice and get enlightenment, based on what I had been reading about in books for so many years. Also, I realized that during my time in Korea, I had never experienced traditional Korean culture, having spent most of my time in the cities. There was one temple near Daejeon with which I felt especially connected, named Shin Won Sa, on Kye Ryong San Mountain. However, the abbot of this temple told me that I could not live there, so instead I rented a small room in a traditional house with two old grandmothers in the village next to the temple.

In the fall of 1995 I moved into this house, which had electricity but no running water or heat, and I began a kind of retreat. During this period I would wake every day around 6:00 A.M. and then walk to the temple next door for an hour of meditation in the famous Mountain

God Shrine. This building looks even older than its one hundred and fifty years and is full of energy from hundreds of pilgrims who have come to worship and meditate there. I saw many people come to bow to the Mountain God, but I looked down on them, not understanding the nature of bowing, as I saw it merely as some superstitious ritual. I was quite attached to this idea of sitting meditation, even though I was not very good at it.

After sitting for an hour, I would return to my house and cook breakfast. In the mornings I would usually take a walk to the top of Kye Ryong Mountain, which is about a three-hour climb, then return, cook my lunch, and spend the afternoon either reading or writing. In the evenings I would spend another hour sitting in the Mountain God Shrine before going to bed.

While I was staying near Shin Won Sa and following this lifestyle, an American monk named Mu Shim Sunim was staying at Shin Won Sa doing a one-hundred-day solo retreat. We didn't have much contact, because Mu Shim Sunim was keeping silence, but I was fascinated by the idea of a Westerner who had left home to become a Buddhist monk. I had become a little disappointed with my personal practice, so I thought I might move to Thailand and find a group of Westerners with whom I could practice meditation.

However, one day as I headed out the door for my regular mountain climb, I was surprised to see a group of Western monks and nuns who had come to Shin Won Sa to help Mu Shim Sunim celebrate the end of his retreat. I talked to one of them, named Chong An Sunim, who gave me some of Dae Soen Sa Nim's basic teachings and suggested that I drop by the International Zen Center at Hwa Gye Sa, a temple in Seoul. Inspired by this meeting, I took advantage of the opportunity and spent a night at

Hwa Gye Sa the next week, when I went up to Seoul to get my visa for Thailand.

This night changed my life. Although I did not meet Zen Master Seung Sahn himself, I had an interview with Do Mun Sunim, who is now called Zen Master Dae Bong. I immediately connected with him and also enjoyed the basic teaching I heard that night, so I abandoned the plan to go to Thailand and decided to shave my head and sit a three-month winter Kyol Che at Hwa Gye Sa as a layman.

This first Kyol Che was the hardest thing I'd ever done in my life. I had never sat in meditation more than an hour at one time, much less attempted a three-month intensive retreat. During this retreat we were rising every morning at three and sitting about eight hours a day, in addition to the formal meals, chanting, interviews, and everything else. For about the first month I was sure I would die. It was a kind of detox, for all of that heavy karma of drug use, drinking, carousing, and sexual desire seemed to bite back with a vengeance during every sitting period.

This physical, mental, and emotional suffering was so intense that during several interviews with Do Mun Sunim I asked him for his advice: How can I survive a three-month Kyol Che? Do Mun Sunim recommended bowing as the number one cure-all for every kind of karmic ailment, so I tried it and soon embraced this new form of practice.

For me, bowing was at first mainly a physical experience, for my body was so tight from sitting and thinking all the time that I needed some sort of release. Thus, as most beginners, I began to bow in a frenzied manner, leaping up and down from the mat as if competing for an Olympic gold medal. This basic physical release helped my sitting on a fundamental level. It freed up my profoundly stuck energy, and it was easier to sit and be still after doing a few hundred bows.

I gradually began to experience the subtle aspects of bowing practice, as I was introduced to the correct breathing method of exhaling long and slow on the way down, and then a shorter inhalation while coming up. I also began to focus on the movement of the body through the whole motion, thus increasing my power of concentration, which in turn helped my sitting practice even more.

After this first retreat I realized the potential power of practicing, but I also realized how hard I would have to work as a practitioner to overcome my mountain of karma and become a clear and compassionate human being. I was fascinated at the prospect of living at a temple that had a real Zen master. I decided to become a *haeng-ja* (the probationary stage before becoming a novice monk), and then one year later a monk, to devote my life to practice.

During the end of my year-long *haeng-ja* training, I attended a three-week boot-camp-style workshop run by the Korean Chogye order. Every *haeng-ja* in Korea attends this workshop before taking the official *sami* (novice monk) precepts. It is somewhat tortuous, as the teachers yell at you constantly and subject you to an army-style training atmosphere, which is supposed to help you cultivate humility.

On the final night of this three-week training, we all did three thousand bows together, while chanting *Sogamuni Bul* (the name of Buddha Sakyamuni in Korean). Imagine the energy of one hundred and fifty male voices, all chanting in unison and prostrating themselves for more than eight hours in a dharma hall. Of course it was painful at times, and I often found myself watching the clock, wondering when it would be over, but after a few hours of this practice the power of the group mind overwhelmed this struggling "small I," and we all bowed together as one. The next morning we took our novice monk's precepts, having cleansed some of our karma with this practice.

After this initial experience with group bowing, I began to join the monthly three thousand bows at Hwa Gye Sa. The last Saturday of every month, almost two hundred lay practitioners assemble in the Great Hall of Nirvana and Light to do this bowing practice together. Most of those assembled are women, and, in the front row, the line of monks leads the assembly with hits on a *chugpi* (a split piece of wood that, when hit, produces a clacking sound). The whole group chants *Kwan Seum Bosal* while bowing, and one is very easily able to put down the poisons of the "small I." This is truly "just do it" practicing, for after so many hours of bowing together, it is almost impossible to hold onto your opinions and condition, so you just bow and chant.

I've performed this all-night, three-thousand-bows practice close to ten times. One particular evening, a year

or two after becoming a monk, I was suffering deeply as I began to bow, questioning my life and wracked by the effects of an unbridled "desire mind." For several hours I was plagued by this stuck energy and uncontrolled thinking, when suddenly, as I prostrated my body on the mat and lifted my hands, it all disappeared. In that moment, there was only that bow and nothing else and everything was complete as it was. For the rest of the evening the bowing seemed to happen by itself, and indeed for the next few days there was an ease of life I had never experienced before.

This kind of "release" is not special, and most people who practice experience it at one point or another. But for practitioners such as myself, recovering intellectuals, overwhelmed by mountains of karma, and suffering the afflictions of the deluded "I," these brief windows of opening are precious. Bowing is a "just do it" practice, and as you bow and bow and bow, slowly your "small I" lets go and you enter the realm of "big I," or "One Mind," or whatever name you have for it.

One famous Zen Master in Korea, Soeng Chol Sunim, prescribed bowing for all his disciples. Anyone who wanted to meet him first had to do three thousand bows before he or she was even allowed an audience with the master. Most of the disciples at his temple still begin their monastic career by completing ten-thousand-bow retreats, sometimes doing ten thousand bows for a week, for up to three months. Soeng Chol Sunim believed that bowing was a basic practice to cleanse one's karma before one could even consider sitting in meditation.

There is a story from the time of Buddha Sakyamuni. The Buddha was walking along the road when he saw a pile of bones. He immediately prostrated himself three times in front of these bones. His followers were astonished that their great master would bow to a bunch of bones, so they asked why he had done this. He responded that these had been the bones of his mother in a previous life.

When we carry this kind of mind, we are able to bow to anyone or anything at any moment. Not wanting to bow shows a holding or attached mind. Bowing to someone or something shows a willingness to surrender to the unknown, to return to "don't know," to give up one's ideas and arrogance. When done with the proper attitude, bowing cultivates humility.

Many Korean people also believe bowing accrues great merit. One Korean monk, while constructing a temple on Cheju Island, did five thousand bows a day for two hundred days, thus completing a one-million-bow retreat. The laypeople were so inspired by his tremendous effort that they donated enough money to build a magnificent temple, called Yak Cheon Sa.

I have now been a monk for six years. During this time I have tried to make bowing an important part of my practice, along with chanting and sitting. At any given time I try to maintain at least five hundred bows a day, and when possible seven hundred or a thousand bows a day. Dae Soen Sa Nim has always taught us to practice bowing, chanting, and sitting together. Each form of practice has its particular strong points, and when they are done in tandem they complement each other.

Last summer I completed a one-hundred-day solo retreat at a small mountain hermitage in the southern part of the Korean peninsula. During this retreat, I started by bowing one thousand five hundred times, then chanting for six hours and sitting for three hours a day. By the last month I had increased to two thousand bows a day, and for the last week I did an intensive session of three thousand bows a day with no sleep, while continuing the regular chanting and sitting schedule nonstop. This was one of the most powerful experiences of my life. During this last week in particular, I experienced incredible energy and clarity that I'd never known before. I attribute this to the bowing practice. The practice of not sleeping for a week is powerful in its own right, but coupled with bowing it is amazing.

More than two years ago, an American monk named Dae Soen Sa Nim and I completed a "three steps, one bow" pilgrimage around Kye Ryong San Mountain. We started at our home temple of Mu Sang Sa, and after nearly two weeks of prostrating ourselves down the road, we completed our trip around the mountain. This is an extremely powerful practice, for you must completely surrender your dignity and humble yourself as you plant your face in the dirt, dead animals, and garbage on the road. Originally these ideas of dirty, clean, high, and low do not exist, and this kind of practice, while difficult at first, allows one to deeply digest this point.

Bowing is a profound spiritual practice anyone can do. The number of bows is not so important—it is more the sincerity of mind with which you do each bow. I've seen ninety-year-old grandmothers come to the temple, and although they perform only three prostrations, the sincere dedication and incredible "try mind" they exhibit is far greater than many people who do hundreds of bows every day. Many monks in Korea are so proud that they will never bow to a nun or layperson. But with sincere bowing, we throw away such distinctions, and when we bow to each other, we are bowing to the True Nature that is identical within us all.

With each of these stories, one of the patterns that emerges is the presence of the past in the here and now. The pilgrimages undertaken by Hung Ju, Hung Yo, and Myong Haeng Sunim bear a direct relationship to the stories and figures from history. We can draw inspiration from our traditions' stories. For each one of the three stories I have included here, there are many others that lie waiting, like precious things, for us to receive as part of our spiritual heritage and to make part of our living tradition by following the examples in those stories.

CHAPTER SEVEN

YOUR OWN BOWING PRACTICE

Some people who read this book may already have a well-developed spiritual practice and a tradition to which they connect. Other people may be looking to deepen their practice, and still others may be searching for a practice or tradition to which they feel a connection. No matter what point we are at in our spiritual paths, we can incorporate bowing into our daily life and practice. In this chapter, we'll explore how to make bowing part of our daily practice.

Spiritual practice can benefit anyone. With a stable and consistent practice, we are able to develop fully our compassion and wisdom. We can grow with our practice and our faith, finding both a personal source of strength and often a supportive community to which we can give and from which we can receive the gifts of a shared practice and tradition. Bowing, as one of the many practices that traditions use to open our hearts and strengthen our spiritual core, has a significant place in our larger practice.

Although it's hardly necessary to belong to one of the major denominations of a world religion to have a strong spiritual life, religious and spiritual traditions do offer us good examples of how to build a strong foundation for our spiritual practice. All major world religions emphasize the need for a direction in our lives and practice, and for an intention to accompany that direction.

Finding our direction means asking ourselves, "Why am I practicing? How does my practice affect me and my situation?" In Zen, our direction is attaining enlightenment and helping others. We practice meditation, morality, generosity, compassion, perseverance, and patience so that we can develop wisdom and compassion. We use bowing as a reminder of our direction and as a way to cultivate our minds and hearts. Other traditions have similar directions and practices to help keep us properly on the path. But we need a direction so that we know why we're acting, and for what reason. Bowing, like other specific practices, helps us keep our direction clear, and our direction gives our bowing purpose and usefulness. Just bowing without direction is only so much physical movement. Without direction, the idea of *metania,* of turning around, is meaningless, because we have nothing we are turning from and nothing we are turning toward.

Intention is the specific way in which our direction manifests itself each day and with each situation. When we look at our lives and our world, what do we see that we—and our world—need? I often chant *"Kwan Seum Bosal,"* the name of the Bodhisattva of Compassion, to help me always keep my intention to be compassionate and my direction to help others clear. In this case, my intention and direction are both compassionate action. I may also chant the mantra of wisdom, *"gate gate paragate parasamgate bodhi svaha"* (gone, gone, gone beyond, gone beyond to enlightenment, so be it) if my intention is to develop wisdom. If I'm angry and trying to develop patience, then my intention is to put down my anger. With all these intentions, my direction is still, "How may I help you?"

Bowing is about relationships. The actual *way* we bow creates a relationship between ourselves and a tradition. Our direction creates a relationship between ourselves and the greater purpose of our lives. Our intention creates a relationship between ourselves and our daily lives. Bowing itself, the physical action, creates a relationship between our inner and outer actions, and it can help us accomplish our intention and practice our direction. A teacher of mine once described prayer as a bridge between intention and action. I would say the same is true of bowing, except that bowing, because it's physical, can spur us to action in a more immediate way because it *is* an action we can take. Bowing can function as a physical prayer and carry us from the thought of doing something to actually doing it.

One of my teachers, Zen Master Dae Kwang, studies both Christianity and Buddhism. He says that Jesus taught, "Pray always," and that the Buddha said there were four times when one should practice meditation—while sitting, standing, walking, or lying down. "Sounds a lot like 'Pray always,' doesn't it?" Dae Kwang says. Jesus, Buddha, and Zen Master Dae Kwang are all pointing to the same thing: we should always be aware and awake in everything we do. We should set aside formal times for practice, both personal practice and practice with a community, but the true fruits of our practice are borne out in our everyday lives, in our every interaction. Our formal practice is our opportunity to really focus and work on ourselves. But the great opportunity to practice begins when we sit down at the breakfast table with our partner, parents, or children; or when we walk into the office and say hello to our coworkers; or when we interact with strangers on the street or in a store. Then we can really put our compassion and wisdom into action.

Setting aside time for practice helps us accomplish this everyday, moment-to-moment wakefulness. Bowing is our bridge between the intentions we have in our formal practice and our daily actions. Our formal practice falls into two broad categories, personal practice and community practice. In our personal practice we can focus on specific aspects of our practice and our lives. Practicing with a community gives us an opportunity to connect with other people and our tradition. Both personal practice and communal practice are important in our spiritual lives. Bowing also has a role in both these aspects of practice, and we'll explore how bowing fits into personal and communal practice next. We should always remember that bowing is as much a mental action as it is a physical action. Whether we do one bow or one million, if we do that one bow with one hundred percent focus, then this is better than all the bows in the world, because we have fully attained the moment. Everyone—Christians, Jews, Muslims, Hindus, Buddhists, anyone from any tradition—can bow with one hundred percent focus in a temple, church, or mosque, with their congregation, or all alone. Whatever our inspiration and whatever our practice, we can do this.

What consistent and repeated practice or worship allows us is the opportunity to come back to the moment and attain this one hundred percent focus. I hope that the tools I have found to be useful as I've built my own practice as a Buddhist are also useful for you. Because I've centered my practice around Buddhism, and Zen Buddhism in particular, my tools have a certain flavor that may not work for you. We should all feel free to experiment a little and adapt these tools and techniques, especially in our personal practice. Because our personal practice is often the most fluid and least formal aspect of our spiritual practice (in comparison to communal practice, which often has a set structure and form to it, which fortunately allows everyone participating to know what will happen next!), we'll first explore how we can use bowing in our personal practice.

GIVING TIME AND CULTIVATING AWARENESS: OUR PERSONAL PRACTICE

What is a "personal practice"? I've found that, for me, "personal practice" often means the times when I'm in solitude—not necessarily alone, however—and I can focus on one specific aspect of my practice. This idea of personal practice exists only in relation to communal practice, and so if we're defining personal practice then we also need to define communal practice. In Zen, we focus on "together action" when we practice as a community, which means working with other people in harmony and supporting one another through that harmony. If we're in the meditation hall, together action means bowing, chanting, and sitting as a group. If we're working around the Zen center, it means everyone works at the same time, not some people working and other people sitting around chatting and drinking tea. So this idea of "together action" doesn't always mean doing exactly the same thing at the same time. It's more like working in harmony. Any time a community gathers together to practice or worship is also "together action." In the liturgical Christian churches, for example, Mass is celebrated with the entire community acting together as people recite prayers and praise and take Communion.

Personal practice isn't disharmonious with community worship. Rather, if we're feeling a need in our practice to, say, do two hundred or three hundred bows, and in the meditation hall when we're practicing with others we can only do one hundred, then our "personal practice" is the time when we do our extra bows, or extra chanting, or extra sitting that we understand we need. Personal practice gives us the opportunity to concentrate our energy on one specific thing. Sometimes we do this alone, sometimes in the midst of many people. Solitude can help us focus, but sometimes the energy of many other people also engaged in personal practice can vitalize our own efforts. Many Christian communities are using contemplative prayer as both a personal and a communal practice. This brings meditation into worship, and also gives us the opportunity to engage in meditation either on our own or as part of a group. This idea of "personal practice" is loose, just like "together action" and "communal practice" are loose. If ten people in a room are all doing "personal practice," but because they get to share their energy with one another and so are working together, then "personal" and "communal" are just relative terms. The relativity of labels aside, there are definitely times when we make the decisions about how we're going to practice and what we're going to focus on during practice. These personal times can be wonderful opportunities to focus on bowing.

One important aspect of practice is consistency. We should find a time each day that we're going to devote to practice. Even if it's only five minutes, having a consistent time set aside for practice can really help us build our spiritual practice. A good time to practice is when we first wake up. Most of us get up at about the same time each day, and it's simple to set our alarm five or ten minutes earlier. Our minds also tend to be clearer in the morning, and starting with practice sets a tone for the rest of the day.

Because bowing is a physical practice, bowing in the morning can also be a great way to wake up physically and spiritually. One of my teachers, a nun from Australia, used to say, "When you hit the floor in the morning, do three bows!" She meant it literally: before uttering a word, before brushing your teeth, before *anything,* you should bow.

Becoming awake and aware are important aspects of any spiritual practice. We can begin with an awareness of our bodies, because our bodies are easy to observe, and as our strength of concentration increases, we'll find this initial awareness of our bodies expands into an awareness of both our external environment and our internal environment of thoughts and emotions. In the Zen tradition, we begin our bows standing, with our feet firmly planted on the floor and our hands at our hearts. This is a strong stance, and it's one that allows us to both stretch and ground our bodies. Before we begin our first bow, we should take a deep breath, and really wake up our bodies. Our breath should go all the way down into our bellies, so that we feel our stomachs and chests rise with our breathing. As we wake up our bodies, we can start to wake up our mind. Be aware of your body. How does it feel? Are your legs tight, is your back stiff, or are you tired? Maybe you feel refreshed and alert. Whatever your physical state, be aware of it. Don't make anything out of it, though—you don't need to think that a stiff back is bad and feeling limber is good. When you're beginning your practice, you just want to be aware. Awareness is without judgment, because it comes before thinking.

After you've maintained an awareness of your body for about ten deep breaths, then you can shift your awareness to your inner state. How do you feel? Are you sad about something? Are you joyful? Whatever your mood, just be aware of it. Again, you don't need to make anything of it, such as being sad is bad and feeling joyful good, or vice versa. Just be aware. This awareness takes time to develop. It's difficult not to get involved in our emotions. If we feel joy, for example, we start thinking about that joy, what happened to make us joyful, and what we want to do next with or because of our joy. All this is "making," and all we need when we practice is *awareness*.

We should try to keep a sharp and strong awareness of our inner state for another ten deep breaths. Then we can set an intention, either spoken or not. The Four Great Vows of Zen are the intention I set before I bow: "Sentient beings are numberless, I vow to save them all; delusions are endless, I vow to cut through them all; the teachings are infinite, I vow to learn them all; the Buddha Way is inconceivable, I vow to attain it." These vows remind all Zen students of their direction: to attain enlightenment and save all sentient beings from suffering, no matter how difficult or impossible the task seems. Muslims also set an intention before they perform their daily prayers, but the intention is silent. We should have an intention before practice, because it clarifies our actions and our direction. Anything that connects you to your greater purpose is helpful: "May I practice patience," "May I bring peace to the world," "May I come closer to God."

When we bow, we can hold our intention in our heart. If we have a specific prayer, then we should say that, either aloud or silently. If we have no specific prayer, then we should hold our intention in our heart and keep our awareness on our actions. Staying aware of our actions and our inner state is challenging— if it weren't, we'd all be Buddhas already! Keeping aware is helpful, though, no matter what our tradition or practice. When we act mindlessly or carelessly, we lose the power of bowing. Bowing is an opportunity to reorient our lives. Spiritual practice gives us many bridges between intention and action. Bowing is one of them.

When we bow, we can put down whatever baggage we have. Our baggage isn't just "bad" baggage, such as a rough day at work or a fight with a friend. We have "good" baggage too, and this can impede us if we get too attached to the good things in our life. We want only the good things and none of the bad things, and we carry around the fear of losing the good. When we bow, we can put all of it down, good and bad. We have our intention, and we just bow.

If your spiritual practice is one that can incorporate Zen-style bowing, that is, formal and repeated bows, then I would encourage you to try it. You can use a formal Zen-style bowing, like the one I described in chapter three, or you can use Tibetan-style bowing, which is less formal, like the one I described in chapter two. Whatever form we use, the important part of the physical bow is to make sure we engage our entire body. If our knees allow it, we should also make sure our head touches the floor. If we need to be kind to our knees, then we can bow from the waist, making sure that we lower our heads, so that we remember humility as we bow. We can bring awareness to any tradition and any practice, and we will benefit.

If we really want to develop our awareness as we bow, then doing sets of bows is helpful. A set of one hundred and eight is a lot of bows, especially if we're just starting. Doing twenty-one, thirty-six, or fifty-four bows at one time is a good way to ease into the practice of bowing. As our physical stamina and mental awareness increase, we can do more bows. We should do them with just enough time for us to keep our breath deep and steady—but it's also okay to get a little out of breath and break a sweat! If we bow too slowly, our mind can wander off. If we bow too quickly, we are always anticipating the next bow instead of actually bowing. So a steady rhythm is important when we bow. Quality matters in spiritual practice. Even if we're strong enough to do three hundred bows, we're better served doing three completely sincere and totally aware bows.

Our formal practice should have a clearly defined beginning and end. By having a beginning and an end, we can set that time aside. If we don't really know when we start and when we end, then if the phone rings we may answer it, interrupting the energy of our efforts. If we know when we've started practice and when we've ended practice, then if the phone rings we can just let it ring and not interrupt our formal practice. Later, after practice, if the phone rings, then we can answer it, because our "everyday" practice requires answering the phone. But we should have an opening and a closing for our formal practice, so that we can focus ourselves.

For me, reciting the Four Great Vows is the beginning, and bowing (and sitting and chanting) are the middle. I end with a silent dedication of my efforts, that whatever good I have accomplished with my practice may help other beings. Our dedication can be something we create ourselves, although I find a verse from a Sanskrit text, *The Guide to the Bodhisattva's Way of Life* by Shantideva, as translated by Stephen Batchelor, to be a beautiful and inspiring dedication: "For as long as space endures, for as long as living beings remain, until then may I too abide to dispel the suffering of the world." A dedication is like an intention: it focuses our specific efforts on the larger direction of our life. The traditional peace prayer of Saint Francis of Assisi is another beautiful dedication:

Lord, make me an instrument of your peace.

Where there is hatred, let me sow love; where there is discord, unity; where there is doubt, faith; where there is error, truth; where there is despair, hope; where there is sadness, joy; where there is darkness, light.

O Lord, grant that I may not so much seek happiness for myself, to be consoled as to console, to be loved as to love, to be understood as to understand.

For it is in giving that we receive, it is in pardoning that we are pardoned, and it is in dying that we are born to eternal life. Amen.

Another beautiful dedication, from the Jewish tradition, comes from the last portion of the *Amidah:*

Grant peace, goodness, and blessing, grace, kindness, and mercy to us and to all of Israel, your People. Bless us, our Father, all of us as one, in the light of your face, for in the light of your face, Adonai our God, You gave us a Torah of life, a love of grace, righteousness, blessing, mercy, life, and peace. You see fit to bless your People Israel at all times, at every hour, with your peace. Blessed are You, Adonai, who blesses his People Israel with peace.

Every tradition has prayers or aspirations we can use for opening or closing our practice. We should find one that we can connect with sincerely, so that we can really digest the spirit of the words and put them into action in our practice and in our lives. If we really want to focus on a particular aspiration, we can recite it while we bow. And if we have a specific tradition that we practice, then we can use the bowing form from that tradition for our personal practice. Having a strong connection to our personal practice is important because then we can really enter into it. When something doesn't feel right, or feels too foreign, we may shy away from it or focus more on the foreignness of the form, instead of just doing it. If we have a tradition that we're already connected to, we probably don't need to go shopping in other traditions to pick out the parts we think might work with our own tradition. Every spiritual tradition has inspiring verses we can use for our intention and dedication, and while not every tradition uses bowing in the same concentrated way that Buddhism and Zen do, all traditions do use bowing and have a form for bowing.

Our personal practice is a wonderful opportunity to explore the different aspects of bowing and find a structure that works for us. The most important thing is to be awake, one hundred percent, as we bow. This one hundred percent focus is enlightenment, faith in God, union with the Divine—everything that spiritual traditions have pointed to throughout the ages as the ultimate goal or direction of human spiritual endeavors. These are not the same and they are not different—if we are one hundred percent awake when we bow. Then, we are just bowing and our direction is clear, whether it's saving all beings, serving God, or understanding the Divine.

TOGETHER ACTION AND LETTING GO: COMMUNAL PRACTICE

Community is another important part of our spiritual practice. A wonderful energy can result from practice with other people. Practice with others helps us see our attachments quickly, because when we're with others we can't control what happens. When we practice alone, we often get to decide what to do and what not to do. If we like something, then we do it; if we don't, we can either not do it or minimize its presence in our practice. But if we're practicing in a community, then we have to let go of our likes and dislikes and just act together with everyone else. This is also a powerful part of practice.

When Zen students bow together, the most senior student or the Zen master sets the pace. I like to do my bows quickly, with a little pause when my head is down. I have my own particular rhythm that I like to use. But my rhythm is rarely the Zen master's rhythm. I can either spend all one hundred and eight bows feeling grouchy and irritated because I can't bow in the way I like, or I can let it go and just bow. I don't always have an easy time letting go of how I want to bow, but just the fact that I have the opportunity to see my likes and dislikes is wonderful! We don't often see our attachments so clearly, and once we see them we can work on putting them down, one bow at a time.

Community also gives us a chance to connect with our tradition. We have the chance to learn more about our history, or ask our teacher or community leader questions. We can share ourselves with others, find support for our practice, and give support to those around us. Community often reminds us of our direction, because ideally everyone in a community shares a common path. We are accountable to our community. We have to live with the commitments we've made, and we are responsible for our actions. Our spiritual communities and friends act as fellow travelers and guides on our path. If we're not doing the right thing, or if we've engaged in wrong actions that violate precepts or vows we've taken, then the people in our community can help us keep our precepts and vows so our direction stays clear and our intention is focused on that direction.

Also, communities have established forms for practice, such as the one hundred and eight bows in the Zen tradition, *salat* in the Muslim tradition, *metania* and genuflection in the Christian traditions, or *davening* in the Jewish tradition. While personal practice at home can often have a degree of spontaneity to it, practicing in a community is more focused on acting together. This means that very little is spontaneous, because we all have to know what will happen next. The formality of community practice is also wonderful, and a good counterbalance to personal practice. Sister Joanne Veillette, who works at a local Catholic parish in my city, says, "There's nothing spontaneous about the community coming together to pray. It's wonderful that we know when to kneel, sit, and stand. There's no clutter. Everything is so ritualized it leaves you free to enter fully into the moment. We are free to enter fully into the mystery we are celebrating."

Being able "to enter fully into the mystery" is being aware, one hundred percent. We don't need to think about how or when to bow when we take part in community practice, and not thinking is wonderful. When we are not thinking, we're just with the moment, the mystery, totally. When we walk into a cathedral and genuflect or bow toward the Sacred Presence, we can put down all our worries and thoughts, and just touch our knees to the ground or lower our heads. When we move forward into God's presence during the *Amidah,* we can let go of our small problems and just step forward. When we say the *takbeer* and bring our hands to our ears, we are no longer listening to the petty nagging voices in our head, but to the voice of God. When we bow to an image of the Buddha or Krishna, we let go of the false distinction between "self" and "other," and just bow to our own Buddha-mind or divine nature. When we do all of these things with other people, then we are even more able to let go of our small and petty minds and act with other members of our community, sharing, awakening, and bowing together.

In Buddhism, there are many analogies used to explain how wisdom and compassion work together in this thing Buddhists call "enlightenment." Compassion is often called *action,* because in order to truly attain compassion we must learn how to act and interact with our world. And then an even more problematic question arises: Does wisdom give birth to compassion, or does compassion give birth to wisdom? Are they different, or the same? The two are often compared to the two wheels of a cart, or the two wings of a bird. But a bird isn't just two wings, nor is a cart two wheels. There's a whole bird, with a body between the wings, something that lifts itself on those wings and flies. No wings, no flight. No body, no flight. So are the wings separate from the bird, or are they the same as the bird?

Trying to divide practice into "personal" and "communal," or "formal" and "informal," is like asking whether compassion and wisdom are the same or different, or whether the wings are different from or the same as a whole bird. It's like asking whether bowing is something that happens with the body or with the mind, or with both or with neither. Divisions such as "personal" and "communal" and "formal" and "informal" are helpful ways for us to organize our time when we're establishing our practice. After a while, the distinctions among these things begin to dissolve. We still understand that when we walk into the meditation hall, we bow to the Buddha and to our fellow practitioners. This is a correct relationship between ourselves and the environment. After still more time, when we are able to practice and bow sincerely, we find our entire world is a meditation hall, temple, church, or similar sacred space. We find ourselves approaching every situation and person in our life with a readiness to put down our pride and attachments and be open, humble, and thankful—whether we put our hands together or not.

I have one more personal story to share about practice and bowing. A woman who comes to the New Haven Zen Center, one of my dharma-sisters, has both of her legs amputated near the knee. She is a completely wonderful, lively, and funny woman. During retreats, when we assemble in the morning to do our one hundred and eight bows, she comes up to the meditation hall and bows with us. It would be easy for her to say, "My not having legs is a hindrance. I can't do a full prostration properly because I'm unable to do the form. I won't come up for bows. I'll wait until the chanting starts." But she comes up, settles herself on her mat, and does all one hundred and eight bows with us, putting her forehead on the mat and her palms up with all of us. This is real together action, and real practice. She has no hindrance to her bowing, because she *just does it*. She isn't attached to form, she isn't attached to how it looks or to not having anything below her knees. What she has gone through is unimaginable. Many of us will never have to face a similar loss. Her strength and willingness to try are incredible and inspirational. When I think of how easily I'm distracted by even momentary things, such as the telephone ringing, and how readily I look for a reason not to get up and practice, I am awed by her strength. If she is willing to try, and even more willing to let go of her attachments, then how can I not also be willing to try and to let go—especially given the temporary nature of most of my hindrances and challenges. If we could all bow like this, just doing it and not being hindered in our practice by anything, especially not our momentary distractions and temporary situations, then we would all be awake!

All this reading is nothing without action. I hope that these words have been informative and helpful. But I hope even more that every reader will put this book down, bow with one hundred percent awareness, and attain her or his goal soon. Just do it!

AFTERWORD

JUST DO IT!

One morning I went out to breakfast with the abbot of the Zen Center, just to chat. Bruce asked me how the writing of this book was going, and I started hemming and hawing, because I tend to feel more ambivalent about my writing the closer I come to finishing a project. Things never seem to go as planned, or I can't get hold of someone I want to interview, or I can't find that book or quote that I was looking for. I always worry that I haven't done justice to my subject. "I should have done more research," I'll say to myself. "I should have revised that section once more, and I forgot to say something about this or that."

I mentioned all this to the abbot over the course of a much longer conversation. Earlier we had been talking about the world situation, with all the wars and epidemics and natural disasters. I told the abbot that the batteries on my radio had given out about a month ago, and since then I hadn't listened to the news or picked up a newspaper. Because the Zen Center doesn't have television, I hadn't watched any news, either. I said, "I figure that there's always someone suffering. I don't have to know about a war or an epidemic to know that there is suffering in the world. If I listen to my friends or my family, or even just to myself, I'll know that there is suffering in the world. I just chant *'Kwan Seum Bosal,'* because someone somewhere needs it. We are never separate from suffering. It doesn't happen 'over there,' someplace else in the world. It happens right here, in our own lives and in our own immediate environment."

Later, when we were talking about this book and I was fumbling through some of my questions about what bowing *really* is, the abbot said, "But you don't have to bend your knees to bow." I'd been making a big deal to myself about *how* we bow, hands together and knees bending and foreheads touching the ground or not touching the ground. How would a Jewish person who bows only at certain times during a service find this book useful? How would a Christian incorporate bowing into traditional Christian prayer? I'd gotten stuck in this idea of Zen bowing, and I was still trying to map Zen-style bowing over other spiritual traditions, without much success.

Bruce said, "I liked what you said earlier about intimacy with suffering—you don't have to watch or read the news to know that there is suffering, and that this suffering isn't far away, but in your own life and my own life right now. Practice is being intimate with suffering. Bowing is also being intimate with suffering. You don't have to bend your knees to bow. You just need to be intimate with suffering. That doesn't necessarily happen with your body."

Ah! I thought. Suffering, embracing suffering, letting suffering go, and attaining great wisdom and compassion . . . this is bowing, too. So many times over the course of researching and writing this book, I've tried to define bowing to myself and to others. I wish instead that I could invite every person who picks up this book to come over to my house, so that we could bow together—then every person would understand the sacred art of bowing, and I wouldn't have to use any words. Because I was exploring some traditions that were unfamiliar to me in order to write about them, I got in the habit of bowing before I sat down

to write. I *shuckled* and *davened,* made grand *metanias* and genu-
flected, bowed in *ruku'* and prostrated in *sujud,* and completed
two "three steps, one bow" pilgrimages across the kitchen and
living room at the Zen Center. I've done each of these practices,
stumbling over Hebrew and Arabic and crossing myself, because
I wanted to become *intimate* with these bowing forms. Someone
else's words on these practices weren't enough. I needed to experience them, but because I'm not Jewish, Christian, Muslim, or
Hindu, I don't have the full flavor of each tradition. What I
found was that bowing in all these traditions was beautiful and
wonderful. Every single form was a useful way for me to put
down my small mind, be aware, and wake up. Bowing certainly
happens with the body. I hope that I've also conveyed that bowing isn't only the body. Our body is a helpful tool for us to use in
our spiritual practice, just as our minds are helpful. But in the
end, we put all this down and let it go.

I've often been told by people who know a little about
Buddhism, but who haven't ever really practiced it, that it seems
like a pessimistic spirituality. "Life is suffering?" they say to me.
"How depressing." But the flip side of suffering is the release
from suffering. Intimacy with suffering doesn't mean to suffer
but to let go of our fears of suffering so that we can awaken great
compassion. That's not depressing or pessimistic. Jesus suffered
terribly on the cross, and yet in his suffering was the release of all
Christians from their suffering. Is that depressing? Intimacy
with suffering doesn't mean that we walk around feeling down,
upset, always weeping because the world is full of war and sickness. To be intimate with suffering is to let go of even our sadness and our joy, to do just what must be done to help everyone
around us. I find this teaching of helping others, of compassion,
in all the world spiritual traditions.

Bowing is a form of being intimate with suffering. And
bowing is just bowing, suffering is just suffering. We put it
down, and we just do it. The marrow of practice is doing it. In

these confusing times, full of distractions and world events and all the ordinary stuff of everyday life—friends, work, cooking dinner, doing laundry—we need to give our actions and lives direction. Spiritual practice helps us with our direction. Bowing helps us attain our direction.

As I wrote this book, I found myself inspired by the sincere faith and practice of the people with whom I talked. My own bowing practice deepened, and as I bowed, my connection to my world and to its needs, all its suffering and joy, also deepened. Letting go of our attachments does not mean that we become emotionally blank. Rather, we become super-attenuated, highly receptive. Our own emotions no longer cloud situations. When someone laughs, we share their joy and laugh, too. When someone weeps, we share their sorrow and cry, too. We become clear. We can help. Laughter and tears come, and we can always say, "How can I help?" without hindrance.

This is the gift of bowing. I hope this book has been helpful to you. I hope we all become clear and compassionate to help ourselves and the world.

A C K N O W L E D G M E N T S

I would like to sincerely thank the following for their generous participation, help, support, and advice:

Myong Haeng Sunim, Rabbi Lina Grazier-Zerbarini, Sister Joanne Villette, Swami Padmapadananda, Swami Vasishtananda, Imam Zaid Shakir, and Bruce Blair.

I would like to gratefully acknowledge my editor, Maura Shaw, who gave me this wonderful opportunity to explore and write about the exploration—and then patiently worked with me to see this project finished.

I would also like to thank my parents, Bill and Maggie, and my sister, Molly, for their love and unwavering support throughout the writing of this book and all my various endeavors; and my partner, Sally, for *her* love and support during this project and the many transitions that accompanied it.

Finally, I would like to thank my kind teachers: Lama Lhondrop, Geshe Tashi, Ven. Renee Fusi, Geshe Tsulga, Acharya Judith Simmer-Brown, Zen Master Dae Kwang, Chong Hae Ji Do Poep Sa Nim, Zen Master Bobby Rhodes, His Holiness the Dalai Lama, and Zen Master Seung Sahn.

Notes

Notes

Notes

Notes

Notes

Notes

Notes

Notes

Notes

About SKYLIGHT PATHS Publishing

SkyLight Paths Publishing is creating a place where people of different spiritual traditions come together for challenge and inspiration, a place where we can help each other understand the mystery that lies at the heart of our existence.

Through spirituality, our religious beliefs are increasingly becoming a part of our lives—rather than *apart* from our lives. While many of us may be more interested than ever in spiritual growth, we may be less firmly planted in traditional religion. Yet, we do want to deepen our relationship to the sacred, to learn from our own as well as from other faith traditions, and to practice in new ways.

SkyLight Paths sees both believers and seekers as a community that increasingly transcends traditional boundaries of religion and denomination—people wanting to learn from each other, *walking together, finding the way.*

We at SkyLight Paths take great care to produce beautiful books that present meaningful spiritual content in a form that reflects the art of making high quality books. Therefore, we want to acknowledge those who contributed to the production of this book.

PRODUCTION
Tim Holtz & Bridgett Taylor

EDITORIAL
Maura D. Shaw & Emily Wichland

COVER DESIGN
Dawn DeVries Sokol, Tempe, Arizona

TEXT DESIGN
Susan Ramundo, SR Desktop Services, Ridge, New York

PRINTING & BINDING
Versa Press, East Peoria, Illinois

Spiritual Biography

The Life of Evelyn Underhill
An Intimate Portrait of the Groundbreaking Author of Mysticism
by *Margaret Cropper;* Foreword by *Dana Greene*

Evelyn Underhill was a passionate writer and teacher who wrote elegantly on mysticism, worship, and devotional life. This is the story of how she made her way toward spiritual maturity, from her early days of agnosticism to the years when her influence was felt throughout the world. 6 x 9, 288 pp, 5 b/w photos, Quality PB, ISBN 1-893361-70-5 **$18.95**

Zen Effects: *The Life of Alan Watts*
by *Monica Furlong*

The first and only full-length biography of one of the most charismatic spiritual leaders of the twentieth century—now back in print!

Through his widely popular books and lectures, Alan Watts (1915–1973) did more to introduce Eastern philosophy and religion to Western minds than any figure before or since. Here is the only biography of this charismatic figure, who served as Zen teacher, Anglican priest, lecturer, academic, entertainer, a leader of the San Francisco renaissance, and author of more than 30 books, including *The Way of Zen, Psychotherapy East and West* and *The Spirit of Zen.*
6 x 9, 264 pp, Quality PB, ISBN 1-893361-32-2 **$16.95**

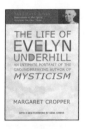
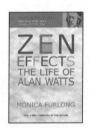

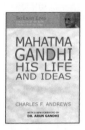

Simone Weil: *A Modern Pilgrimage*
by *Robert Coles*

The extraordinary life of the spiritual philosopher who's been called both saint and madwoman.

The French writer and philosopher Simone Weil (1906–1943) devoted her life to a search for God—while avoiding membership in organized religion. Robert Coles' intriguing study of Weil details her short, eventful life, and is an insightful portrait of the beloved and controversial thinker whose life and writings influenced many (from T. S. Eliot to Adrienne Rich to Albert Camus), and continue to inspire seekers everywhere. 6 x 9, 208 pp, Quality PB, ISBN 1-893361-34-9 **$16.95**

Mahatma Gandhi: *His Life and Ideas*
by *Charles F. Andrews;* Foreword by *Dr. Arun Gandhi*

An intimate biography of one of the greatest social and religious reformers of the modern world.

Examines from a contemporary Christian activist's point of view the religious ideas and political dynamics that influenced the birth of the peaceful resistance movement, the primary tool that Gandhi and the people of his homeland would use to gain India its freedom from British rule. An ideal introduction to the life and life's work of this great spiritual leader.
6 x 9, 336 pp, Quality Paperback, ISBN 1-893361-89-6 **$18.95**

Spiritual Practice

Women Pray
Voices through the Ages, from Many Faiths, Cultures, and Traditions
Edited and with introductions by *Monica Furlong*

Many ways—new and old—to communicate with the Divine.

This beautiful gift book celebrates the rich variety of ways women around the world have called out to the Divine—with words of joy, praise, gratitude, wonder, petition, longing, and even anger—from the ancient world up to our own time. Prayers from women of nearly every religious or spiritual background give us an eloquent expression of what it means to communicate with God.
5 x7¼, 256 pp, Deluxe HC with ribbon marker, ISBN 1-893361-25-X **$19.95**

Praying with Our Hands: *Twenty-One Practices of Embodied Prayer from the World's Spiritual Traditions*
by *Jon M. Sweeney*; Photographs by *Jennifer J. Wilson*;
Foreword by *Mother Tessa Bielecki*; Afterword by *Taitetsu Unno, Ph.D.*

A spiritual guidebook for bringing prayer into our bodies.

This inspiring book of reflections and accompanying photographs shows us twenty-one simple ways of using our hands to speak to God, to enrich our devotion and ritual. All express the various approaches of the world's religious traditions to bringing the body into worship. Spiritual traditions represented include Anglican, Sufi, Zen, Roman Catholic, Yoga, Shaker, Hindu, Jewish, Pentecostal, Eastern Orthodox, and many others.
8 x 8, 96 pp, 22 duotone photographs, Quality PB, ISBN 1-893361-16-0 **$16.95**

   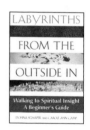

The Sacred Art of Listening
Forty Reflections for Cultivating a Spiritual Practice
by *Kay Lindahl*; Illustrations by *Amy Schnapper*

More than ever before, we need to embrace the skills and practice of listening. You will learn to: Speak clearly from your heart • Communicate with courage and compassion • Heighten your awareness for deep listening • Enhance your ability to listen to people with different belief systems. 8 x 8, 160 pp, Illus., Quality PB, ISBN 1-893361-44-6 **$16.95**

Labyrinths from the Outside In
Walking to Spiritual Insight—a Beginner's Guide
by *Donna Schaper* and *Carole Ann Camp*

The user-friendly, interfaith guide to making and using labyrinths— for meditation, prayer, and celebration.

Labyrinth walking is a spiritual exercise *anyone* can do. This accessible guide unlocks the mysteries of the labyrinth for all of us, providing ideas for using the labyrinth walk for prayer, meditation, and celebrations to mark the most important moments in life. Includes instructions for making a labyrinth of your own and finding one in your area.
6 x 9, 208 pp, b/w illus. and photographs, Quality PB, ISBN 1-893361-18-7 **$16.95**

SkyLight Illuminations Series
Andrew Harvey, series editor

Offers today's spiritual seeker an enjoyable entry into the great classic texts of the world's spiritual traditions. Each classic is presented in an accessible translation, with facing pages of guided commentary from experts, giving you the keys you need to understand the history, context, and meaning of the text. This series enables readers of all backgrounds to experience and understand classic spiritual texts directly, and to make them a part of their lives. Andrew Harvey writes the foreword to each volume, an insightful, personal introduction to each classic.

Bhagavad Gita: *Annotated & Explained*
Translation by *Shri Purohit Swami*; Annotation by *Kendra Crossen Burroughs*

"The very best Gita for first-time readers." —Ken Wilber

Millions of people turn daily to India's most beloved holy book, whose universal appeal has made it popular with non-Hindus and Hindus alike. This edition introduces you to the characters; explains references and philosophical terms; shares the interpretations of famous spiritual leaders and scholars; and more. 5½ x 8½, 192 pp, Quality PB, ISBN 1-893361-28-4 **$16.95**

 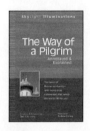 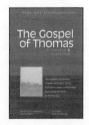

The Way of a Pilgrim: *Annotated & Explained*
Translation and annotation by *Gleb Pokrovsky*

The classic of Russian spirituality—now with facing-page commentary that illuminates and explains the text for you.

This delightful account is the story of one man who sets out to learn the prayer of the heart— also known as the "Jesus prayer"—and how the practice transforms his existence. This edition guides you through an abridged version of the text with facing-page annotations explaining the names, terms and references. 5½ x 8½, 160 pp, Quality PB, ISBN 1-893361-31-4 **$14.95**

The Gospel of Thomas: *Annotated & Explained*
Translation and annotation by *Stevan Davies*

The recently discovered mystical sayings of Jesus—now with facing-page commentary that illuminates and explains the text for you.

Discovered in 1945, this collection of aphoristic sayings sheds new light on the origins of Christianity and the intriguing figure of Jesus, portraying the Kingdom of God as a present fact about the world, rather than a future promise or future threat. This edition guides you through the text with annotations that focus on the meaning of the sayings, ideal for readers with no previous background in Christian history or thought.
5½ x 8½, 192 pp, Quality PB, ISBN 1-893361-45-4 **$16.95**

SkyLight Illuminations Series
Andrew Harvey, series editor

Zohar: *Annotated & Explained*
Translation and annotation by *Daniel C. Matt*

The cornerstone text of Kabbalah.

The best-selling author of *The Essential Kabbalah* brings together in one place the most important teachings of the *Zohar*, the canonical text of Jewish mystical tradition. Guides you step by step through the midrash, mystical fantasy and Hebrew scripture that make up the *Zohar*, explaining the inner meanings in facing-page commentary. Ideal for readers without any prior knowledge of Jewish mysticism.
5½ x 8½, 176 pp, Quality PB, ISBN 1-893361-51-9 **$15.95**

Selections from the Gospel of Sri Ramakrishna
Annotated & Explained
Translation by *Swami Nikhilananda*; Annotation by *Kendra Crossen Burroughs*

The words of India's greatest example of God-consciousness and mystical ecstasy in recent history.

Introduces the fascinating world of the Indian mystic and the universal appeal of his message that has inspired millions of devotees for more than a century. Selections from the original text and insightful yet unobtrusive commentary highlight the most important and inspirational teachings. Ideal for readers without any prior knowledge of Hinduism.
5½ x 8½, 240 pp, b/w photographs, Quality PB, ISBN 1-893361-46-2 **$16.95**

Dhammapada: *Annotated & Explained*
Translation by *Max Müller* and revised by *Jack Maguire*; Annotation by *Jack Maguire*

The classic of Buddhist spiritual practice.

The Dhammapada—words spoken by the Buddha himself over 2,500 years ago—is notoriously difficult to understand for the first-time reader. Now you can experience it with understanding even if you have no previous knowledge of Buddhism. Enlightening facing-page commentary explains all the names, terms, and references, giving you deeper insight into the text.
5½ x 8½, 160 pp, Quality PB, ISBN 1-893361-42-X **$14.95**

Hasidic Tales: *Annotated & Explained*
Translation and annotation by *Rabbi Rami Shapiro*

The legendary tales of the impassioned Hasidic rabbis.

The allegorical quality of Hasidic tales can be perplexing. Here, they are presented as stories rather than parables, making them accessible and meaningful. Each demonstrates the spiritual power of unabashed joy, offers lessons for leading a holy life, and reminds us that the Divine can be found in the everyday. Annotations explain theological concepts, introduce major characters, and clarify references unfamiliar to most readers.
5½ x 8½, 224 pp, Quality PB, ISBN 1-893361-86-1 **$16.95**

Meditation

Meditation without Gurus: *A Guide to the Heart of Practice*
by *Clark Strand*

A straightfoward guide that sets meditation free from pretension and intimidation.

Stripping meditation down to its essential heart—simplicity, lightness, and peace—Clark Strand shows readers how to welcome meditation into their lives without stress, worries, and unreasonable expectations. Includes easy-to-understand exercises.

5½ x 8½ 160 pp, Quality PB, ISBN 1-893361-93-4 **$16.95**

Three Gates to Meditation Practice
A Personal Journey into Sufism, Buddhism, and Judaism
by *David A. Cooper*

Shows us how practicing within more than one spiritual tradition can lead us to our true home.

Here are over fifteen years from the journey of "post-denominational rabbi" David A. Cooper, author of *God Is a Verb*, and his wife, Shoshana—years in which the Coopers explored a rich variety of practices, from chanting Sufi *dhikr* to Buddhist Vipassanā meditation, to the study of Kabbalah and esoteric Judaism. Their experience demonstrates that the spiritual path is really completely within our reach, whoever we are, whatever we do—as long as we are willing to practice it.

5½ x 8½, 240 pp, Quality PB, ISBN 1-893361-22-5 **$16.95**

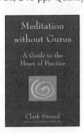 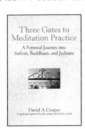  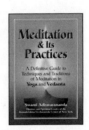

Silence, Simplicity & Solitude
A Complete Guide to Spiritual Retreat at Home
by *David A. Cooper*

The classic personal spiritual retreat guide that enables readers to create their own self-guided spiritual retreat at home.

Award-winning author David Cooper traces personal mystical retreat in all of the world's major traditions, describing the varieties of spiritual practices for modern spiritual seekers. Cooper shares the techniques and practices that encompass the personal spiritual retreat experience, allowing readers to enhance their meditation practices and create an effective, self-guided spiritual retreat in their own homes—without the instruction of a meditation teacher.

5½ x 8½, 336 pp, Quality PB, ISBN 1-893361-04-7 **$16.95**

Meditation & Its Practices
A Definitive Guide to Techniques and Traditions of Meditation in Yoga and Vedanta
by *Swami Adiswarananda*

In one comprehensive and inspiring volume, illuminates for us the principles of the Yoga and Vedanta meditation traditions, the meaning of meditation, its goal of Self-Knowledge, the methods by which concentration is developed, and the ways of achieving self-control. Defines key concepts in clear terms; includes glossary, index.

6 x 9, 504 pp, HC, ISBN 1-893361-83-7 **$34.95**

Children's Spirituality

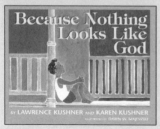

Because Nothing Looks Like God
by *Lawrence and Karen Kushner*
Full-color illus. by
Dawn W. Majewski

For ages 4 & up

Multicultural, Nondenominational, Nonsectarian

Real-life examples of happiness and sadness—from goodnight stories, to the hope and fear felt the first time at bat, to the closing moments of life—introduce children to the possibilities of spiritual life. A vibrant way for children—and their adults—to explore what, where, and how God is in our lives. 11 x 8½, 32 pp, HC,

Full-color illus., ISBN 1-58023-092-X **$16.95**

*Also available: **Teacher's Guide**, 8½ x 11, 22 pp, PB, ISBN 1-58023-140-3* **$6.95** For ages 5–8

Where Is God? (A Board Book)
by *Lawrence and Karen Kushner*; Full-color illus. by *Dawn W. Majewski*

For ages 0–4

A gentle way for young children to explore how God is with us every day, in every way. Abridged from *Because Nothing Looks Like God* by Lawrence and Karen Kushner and specially adapted to board book format to delight and inspire young readers.
5 x 5, 24 pp, Board, Full-color illus., ISBN 1-893361-17-9 **$7.95**

What Does God Look Like? (A Board Book)
by *Lawrence and Karen Kushner*; Full-color illus. by *Dawn W. Majewski*

For ages 0–4

A simple way for young children to explore the ways that we "see" God. Abridged from *Because Nothing Looks Like God* by Lawrence and Karen Kushner and specially adapted to board book format to delight and inspire young readers.
5 x 5, 24 pp, Board, Full-color illus., ISBN 1-893361-23-3 **$7.95**

How Does God Make Things Happen? (A Board Book)
by *Lawrence and Karen Kushner*; Full-color illus. by *Dawn W. Majewski*

For ages 0–4

A charming invitation for young children to explore how God makes things happen in our world. Abridged from *Because Nothing Looks Like God* by Lawrence and Karen Kushner and specially adapted to board book format to delight and inspire young readers.
5 x 5, 24 pp, Board, Full-color illus., ISBN 1-893361-24-1 **$7.95**

What Is God's Name? (A Board Book)
by *Sandy Eisenberg Sasso*; Full-color illus. by *Phoebe Stone*

For ages 0–4

Everyone and everything in the world has a name. What is God's name? Abridged from the award-winning *In God's Name* by Sandy Eisenberg Sasso and specially adapted to board book format to delight and inspire young readers.
5 x 5, 24 pp, Board, Full-color illus., ISBN 1-893361-10-1 **$7.95**

Children's Spirituality

Ten Amazing People
And How They Changed the World
by *Maura D. Shaw*; Foreword by *Dr. Robert Coles*
Full-color illus. by *Stephen Marchesi*

For ages 6–10

Black Elk • Dorothy Day • Malcolm X • Mahatma Gandhi •
Martin Luther King, Jr. • Mother Teresa • Janusz Korczak •
Desmond Tutu • Thich Nhat Hanh • Albert Schweitzer

This vivid, inspirational, and authoritative book will open new possibilities for children by telling the stories of how ten of the past century's greatest leaders changed the world in important ways.
8½ x 11, 48 pp, HC, Full-color illus., ISBN 1-893361-47-0 **$17.95**

God's Paintbrush
by *Sandy Eisenberg Sasso*; Full-color illus. by *Annette Compton*

For ages 4 & up

Invites children of all faiths and backgrounds to encounter God openly in their own lives. Wonderfully interactive; provides questions adult and child can explore together at the end of each episode. "An excellent way to honor the imaginative breadth and depth of the spiritual life of the young." —Dr. Robert Coles, Harvard University
11 x 8½, 32 pp, HC, Full-color illus., ISBN 1-879045-22-2 **$16.95**

Also available:
A Teacher's Guide 8½ x 11, 32 pp, PB, ISBN 1-879045-57-5 **$8.95**
God's Paintbrush Celebration Kit 9½ x 12, HC, Includes 5 sessions/40 full-color Activity Sheets and Teacher Folder with complete instructions, ISBN 1-58023-050-4 **$21.95**

In God's Name
by *Sandy Eisenberg Sasso*; Full-color illus. by *Phoebe Stone*

For ages 4 & up

Like an ancient myth in its poetic text and vibrant illustrations, this award-winning modern fable about the search for God's name celebrates the diversity and, at the same time, the unity of all the people of the world. "What a lovely, healing book!" —Madeleine L'Engle
9 x 12, 32 pp, HC, Full-color illus., ISBN 1-879045-26-5 **$16.95**

Also available in Spanish:
El nombre de Dios 9 x 12, 32 pp, HC, Full-color illus., ISBN 1-893361-63-2 **$16.95**

Where Does God Live?
by *August Gold* and *Matthew J. Perlman*

For ages 3–6

Using simple, everyday examples that children can relate to, this colorful book helps young readers develop a personal understanding of God.
10 x 8½, 32 pp, Quality PB, Full-color photo illus., ISBN 1-893361-39-X **$8.95**

Spirituality

Journeys of Simplicity
Traveling Light with Thomas Merton, Bashō, Edward Abbey, Annie Dillard & Others
by *Philip Harnden*

There is a more graceful way of traveling through life.

Offers vignettes of forty "travelers" and the few ordinary things they carried with them—from place to place, from day to day, from birth to death. What Thoreau took to Walden Pond. What Thomas Merton packed for his final trip to Asia. What Annie Dillard keeps in her writing tent. What an impoverished cook served M. F. K. Fisher for dinner. Much more.

"'How much should I carry with me?' is the quintessential question for any journey, especially the journey of life. Herein you'll find sage, sly, wonderfully subversive advice."
—Bill McKibben, author of *The End of Nature* and *Enough*
5 x 7¼, 128 pp, HC, ISBN 1-893361-76-4 **$16.95**

The Alphabet of Paradise
An A–Z of Spirituality for Everyday Life
by *Howard Cooper*

"An extraordinary book." —Karen Armstrong

One of the most eloquent new voices in spirituality, Howard Cooper takes us on a journey of discovery—into ourselves and into the past—to find the signposts that can help us live more meaningful lives. In twenty-six engaging chapters—from A to Z—Cooper spiritually illuminates the subjects of daily life, using an ancient Jewish mystical method of interpretation that reveals both the literal and more allusive meanings of each. Topics include: Awe, Bodies, Creativity, Dreams, Emotions, Sports, and more.
5 x 7¾, 224 pp, Quality PB, ISBN 1-893361-80-2 **$16.95**

Winter
A Spiritual Biography of the Season
Edited by *Gary Schmidt* and *Susan M. Felch;* Illustrations by *Barry Moser*

Explore how the dormancy of winter can be a time of spiritual preparation and transformation.

In thirty stirring pieces, *Winter* delves into the varied feelings that winter conjures in us, calling up both the barrenness and the beauty of the natural world in wintertime. Includes selections by Will Campbell, Rachel Carson, Annie Dillard, Donald Hall, Ron Hansen, Jane Kenyon, Jamaica Kincaid, Barry Lopez, Kathleen Norris, John Updike, E. B. White, and many others.

"This outstanding anthology features top-flight nature and spirituality writers on the fierce, inexorable season of winter.... Remarkably lively and warm, despite the icy subject."
—★*Publishers Weekly* Starred Review
6 x 9, 288 pp, 6 b/w illus., Quality PB w/ flaps, ISBN 1-893361-92-6 **$18.95**
HC, ISBN 1-893361-53-5 **$21.95**

Religious Etiquette/Reference

How to Be a Perfect Stranger, 3rd Edition
The Essential Religious Etiquette Handbook
Edited by *Stuart M. Matlins* and *Arthur J. Magida*

The indispensable guidebook to help the well-meaning guest when visiting other people's religious ceremonies.

A straightforward guide to the rituals and celebrations of the major religions and denominations in the United States and Canada from the perspective of an interested guest of any other faith, based on information obtained from authorities of each religion. Belongs in every living room, library, and office.

COVERS:

African American Methodist Churches • Assemblies of God • Baha'i • Baptist • Buddhist • Christian Church (Disciples of Christ) • Christian Science (Church of Christ, Scientist) • Churches of Christ • Episcopalian and Anglican • Hindu • Islam • Jehovah's Witnesses • Jewish • Lutheran • Mennonite/Amish • Methodist • Mormon (Church of Jesus Christ of Latter-day Saints) • Native American/First Nations • Orthodox Churches • Pentecostal Church of God • Presbyterian • Quaker (Religious Society of Friends) • Reformed Church in America/Canada • Roman Catholic • Seventh-day Adventist • Sikh • Unitarian Universalist • United Church of Canada • United Church of Christ

6 x 9, 432 pp, Quality PB, ISBN 1-893361-67-5 **$19.95**

Also available:

The Perfect Stranger's Guide to Funerals and Grieving Practices
A Guide to Etiquette in Other People's Religious Ceremonies
Edited by *Stuart M. Matlins*
6 x 9, 240 pp, Quality PB, ISBN 1-893361-20-9 **$16.95**

The Perfect Stranger's Guide to Wedding Ceremonies
A Guide to Etiquette in Other People's Religious Ceremonies
Edited by *Stuart M. Matlins*
6 x 9, 208 pp, Quality PB, ISBN 1-893361-19-5 **$16.95**

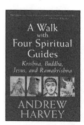